BODY WISDOM
Through
SOMATIC THERAPY

By Grace Bailey

Simple Steps to Manage Stress, Rebuild Resilience,
Cultivate Inner Peace, Rise Above Trauma,
and Enhance the Mind-Body Connection

Published by Bailey Premier Publishing LLC
Canadian, Texas 79014

ISBN 978-1-966543-04-6 Paperback
ISBN 978-1-966543-00-8 Electronic Book Text (Kindle/Epub)
ISBN 978-1-966543-05-3 Hardback
ISBN 978-1-966543-03-9 Audio

Disclaimer:

The author is not a licensed or certified practitioner of Somatic Therapy. The exercises and practices shared in this book are based on personal experience and the positive results achieved through their use. This book is intended for educational and informational purposes only and should not be considered professional medical or therapeutic advice. Please consult a licensed healthcare professional before beginning any new therapeutic or exercise regimen, especially if you have any medical conditions or concerns.

Legal Notice:

The author and publisher of this book disclaim any liability for any injury, loss, or damage resulting from the use or misuse of the information contained within. The content provided is not a substitute for professional care, and all readers are encouraged to seek advice from a qualified healthcare provider. By using the exercises and information in this book, you acknowledge that you are participating at your own risk and accept full responsibility for any outcomes.

CONTENTS

INTRODUCTION

A FEW YEARS AGO, I found myself at a crossroads. I felt stuck emotionally, physically, and spiritually. Being raised in the Bible Belt, I have spent my entire life surrounded by Christian influences and attending various churches. While there were many rewarding and miraculous events throughout that time, I still felt that key elements were missing.

On my birthday in 2020, I felt strongly led to step away from all that I had done in the past and begin a personal sabbatical. The scripture that was the foundation for this change is Romans 8:19: *"All creation is eagerly awaiting the revealing of the sons of God."* I felt like my instructions were to go find out what that meant.

Soon after starting the sabbatical, I met Taylor Remington. He has an online class, "Christian Mysticism and Spirituality plus Rooakh Meditation." His website is www.rooakh.com. As I began working with him, we did breathing and muscle stretching exercises during the meditation portion of the class. Visualization techniques were also an integral part of the teaching. Learning these techniques is the catalyst for this book.

While the term "Somatic Therapy" was never used in these classes, there is no question that the techniques I learned through Taylor's classes are precisely what Somatic Therapy is.

This Somatic Therapy proved to be a catalyst for transformation. It led me to rediscover the wisdom of my body, grounding me and enhancing my resilience. I felt like I was moving forward again physically, emotionally and spiritually. Stress became more manageable, as if I had unlocked a new language my body had been speaking all along, a language I had never learned to understand.

This book, *'Body Wisdom Through Somatic Therapy,'* is not just a collection of techniques. It's a compassionate guide, born from my personal journey, to help you reconnect with your inner wisdom through Somatic Therapy. It offers simple, practical steps to manage stress, rebuild resilience, and enhance the whole body awareness. Consider it more than a book; it's an invitation to a journey of self-discovery and healing.

Somatic Therapy is a holistic approach that focuses on the connection between the mind and body. I realized that you can have a holistic approach and still be a Christian. In fact, God has a characteristic of being holistic. Somatic Therapy involves practices that help you become more aware of your bodily sensations and how they relate to your emotions and thoughts. And you as a whole are composed of your body, mind/soul, and spirit. The awareness of mind and body is crucial to our existences because our bodies hold onto stress and trauma in ways that our minds may not fully understand. By tuning into our bodies, we can release this stored tension and promote balanced well-being.

Over the past four years, using these techniques has profoundly impacted my life. It has given me the tools to face challenges with greater ease and confidence. It has helped me cultivate inner peace and a deeper connection to myself. This journey has inspired me to share what I've learned with others. Everyone can heal and thrive, and Somatic Therapy can be a powerful tool in that process.

You might be wondering how this journey has influenced my Christian faith and background. At first, I wasn't sure what to expect, but I've come to realize that practicing Somatic Therapy has deepened my connection with God—the One in whose image I am created—more than ever before. Now, somatic therapy feels completely natural to me. In the past, I would dismiss my body's sensations, even feeling frustrated or resentful toward it for the pain it carried. But today, I approach my body with kindness and compassion, taking the time to listen and understand its messages. Instead of ignoring it, I engage in an ongoing dialogue with my body. Surely, there is nothing in my faith that would stand against this.

The word that I have used many times to describe this journey has been "rich," and my spiritual connection with the Source of All Life is simply that— much richer. As I have developed a greater understanding about this body that is "fearfully and wonderfully made," my closeness to God has only deepened and I am more sensitive to seeing/feeling and hearing God throughout my daily life. Because of my increased ability to feel again, promptings I receive from the Holy Spirit (my spirit guide) are more noticeable and easier to follow.

What This Book is All About

This book's vision is clear: to empower you with practical steps and easy-to-follow exercises that can be seamlessly integrated into your daily life. It's a comprehensive resource, including a variety of bodily exercises designed to help you manage stress, rebuild resilience, and enhance your mind-body connection. It is also my prayer that this book can be a bridge between the Christian world and the holistic healing therapies outlined in this book.

you are new to Somatic Therapy or have some experience, this book offers valuable insights and practices to support your growth and well-being.

This book's structure is designed to guide you through your Somatic Therapy journey step by step. Each chapter focuses on a different aspect of Somatic Therapy, from understanding the basics to exploring specific techniques for stress management and renewed coping skills. Throughout the book, you'll encounter exercises, reflections, and journaling prompts designed to help you apply what you've learned and track your progress.

As you begin this journey, I encourage you to approach it with an open mind and a compassionate heart. Somatic Therapy techniques do not in any way invoke evil spirits, channel anything, or set you up for sin unless you specifically engage in these during the exercises. Healing can integrate your body, mind and spirit. It is not always a linear process, and it is essential to be gentle with yourself along the way. I invite you to explore the practices in this book and see how they resonate with you. Remember that you have the wisdom within you to heal and thrive. Uncover a new level of connection to this wonderful and fearfully made body that you have.

Let's take this journey together. Let's reconnect with our bodies, manage stress, and cultivate inner peace. The path to healing and resilience is within reach and starts with a single step. Welcome to *"Body Wisdom Through Somatic Therapy."* Your journey begins now.

Chapter 1

UNDERSTANDING
SOMATIC THERAPY

*Your body is the most complete and miraculous
piece of technology you will ever own.*

-- *UNKNOWN*

What is Somatic Therapy?

To START off, you'LL have to know what Somatic Therapy (ST) is. Somatic Therapy is part of a holistic approach to health that emphasizes the connection between the mind and body. "Somatic" comes from the Greek word soma, meaning "body," so you could easily substitute the phrase "body therapy" for Somatic Therapy if that makes it easier to grasp the concepts.

In modern usage, "somatic" refers to anything related to the body, especially as distinct from the mind. In the context of therapy or health, somatic often refers to the body's role in emotional and psychological experiences and emphasizes the connection between the mind and physical sensations.

Usually, therapies that address the mind––such as counseling, psychology, and psychiatry––"talk out" what is going on for the patient receiving the therapy. Traditional talk therapy focuses primarily on verbal communication and what's happening inside the person's mind via their thoughts; the cognitive processes. The person is usually on a couch or in a very comfortable chair. The interaction is primarily through the words spoken.

Somatic Therapy may also occur with someone in a comfortable chair, and certainly there will be verbal communication about what's happening inside their mind but the therapist is doing a lot more. The therapist is looking for cues from the body that stress is present. This may show up in the person's muscles anywhere in their body. Once these are identified, the patient can tune into the body sensations and find the treasure that they hold.

ST recognizes that our bodies hold onto stress, trauma, and unresolved emotions, which can manifest as physical sensations. By tuning into these sensations, we can begin to process and release the emotional weights they carry. The end result of the session is that the emotional burdens once held have been let go. There's a lightness that comes to the person who now doesn't feel as if he or she is carrying the weight of the world anymore.

Somatic practice can be taught so that it no longer needs a therapist. It helps cultivate a deeper awareness of your body, allowing you to understand and respond to its signals more effectively.

The Roots of Somatic Therapy

The origins of Somatic Therapy can be traced back to the work of Wilhelm Reich, a pioneering psychoanalyst who studied under Sigmund Freud. Reich developed a concept called "character analysis," focusing on how physical expressions and behaviors reflect psychological defenses. He introduced the idea that muscular tension, or "armoring," is a physical manifestation of emotional repression.

Here's an example of this: When watching a scary movie, do you find yourself tensing your neck and back? This would be an example of what Reich was finding and reporting on. The muscle tension is, in a way, preventing what is being watched from entering totally into the body. It is also preventing the person from expressing emotions about what is watched.

Reich's 'radical' ideas led to his expulsion from the psychoanalytic community, but his influence persisted. Alexander Lowen, a student of Reich, further developed these concepts into bioenergetics, a therapeutic approach that combines physical exercises with emotional exploration.

Another key figure in the field, Peter Levine, created Somatic Experiencing, a therapeutic method specifically designed to address trauma. Levine's work emphasized the importance of understanding how trauma impacts the nervous system and how bodily sensations can guide the healing process. These pioneers laid the groundwork for a variety of Somatic Therapy modalities, each offering unique techniques to help individuals heal through body awareness.

Somatic Therapy Fundamental Principles

At its core, Somatic Therapy is guided by several fundamental principles. First, it recognizes that the body holds memories of trauma. These memories can manifest as physical sensations, such as tension, pain, or numbness.

I'm reminded of a woman now in her 40s who tenses up in her entire back if someone lightly touches her back. Although I do not know the specifics of her case, one can deduce that the mere act of touch triggers a previous trauma. Her tenseness is a clue to armoring and emotional repression surrounding the incident. It's possible that ST could offer a breakthrough here for this woman. A therapist would help her identify the feelings and even flashbacks she may be experiencing, and they can be "processed," giving her a sense of relief and freedom.

Healing from trauma involves integrating these physical sensations with emotional processing, allowing the release of stored trauma and newfound relief.

Another critical principle about ST is the importance of a safe therapeutic environment. Creating a space where you feel secure and supported is essential for effective healing. This environment allows you to explore your bodily sensations without fear, fostering a sense of trust and openness.

You can see from the definition of Somatic Therapy that there is no conflict of interest between any type of philosophical or religious beliefs one has and what these therapies are or do. They simply address what is happening with the body and its interrelationship with one's thoughts, feelings, and behaviors. They don't address religion on any level.

The Five Major Types of Somatic Therapy

There are several types of Somatic Therapy, each offering different techniques and approaches.

- Peter Levine developed **Somatic Experiencing**, which focuses on helping individuals become aware of their bodily sensations and use this awareness to release trauma.

- Alexander Lowen created **Bioenergetics**, which combines physical exercises with emotional exploration to help individuals overcome physical and emotional blockages.

- The **Hakomi Method** integrates Mindfulness and Body Awareness to uncover and transform unconscious patterns.

- **Sensorimotor Psychotherapy** combines Somatic Therapy with traditional talk therapy to address the physical and emotional aspects of trauma.

- The **Feldenkrais Method** uses gentle movements to improve body awareness and function, helping individuals mindfully reconnect with their bodies.

In this book, we will focus on Somatic Experiencing, Bioenergetics, and Sensorimotor Psychotherapy.

In summary, Somatic Therapy is a powerful approach that emphasizes the mind-body connection that we all have as part of our make-up. By becoming more aware of bodily sensations and understanding how they relate to your emotions and thoughts, you can begin to release stored trauma and promote balanced well-being.

The Science Behind Somatic Therapy

Let's delve a little deeper into Somatic Therapy's history, principles, and types, for a more comprehensive understanding of this transformative practice.

The science behind ST is briefly touched on here, but Chapter 9 provides a more in-depth discussion if you want to explore it further.

You may have heard or read the term, "the neurobiology of trauma" on internet articles. What does this mean? It means the study of how trauma affects the brain and nervous system––the brain structures involved, the fight, flight, or freeze response, the memory and trauma relationship, and the long-term effects of the trauma.

Understanding the neurobiology of trauma is key to grasping why Somatic Therapy is so effective. Trauma doesn't just reside in our minds; it deeply affects our bodies and brains. With a comprehension about trauma and ST techniques, you will be able to alter many things in your life. So let's start with the two different parts of the brain that are critical for response to trauma: the amygdala and the hippocampus.

The amygdala, often called the brain's alarm system, plays a crucial role here.

When we encounter something that is threatening, our brain's amygdala signals danger, triggering the fight-flight-freeze response. This is where our autonomic nervous system (ANS) comes into play, preparing our bodies to either confront the threat, escape it, or freeze in place. The ANS works automatically without conscious control of it.

The hippocampus, another vital part of the brain, helps us process and store these traumatic memories.

Your amygdala responds to stress. This picture depicts how what you see will affect different parts of your brain.

However, during overwhelming events, the hippocampus can become impaired, making it difficult to integrate these memories properly. This leaves us with fragmented, distressing recollections that resurface unexpectedly, causing us to relive the trauma.

In 2020, German scientists wrote a scientific paper on how the architecture and cells of the dentate gyrus in the hippocampus can alter cognition. Various combinations of these cells affect the encoding, retrieval, and discrimination of similar memories.

This finding is particularly relevant to the neurobiology of trauma because the dentate gyrus plays a crucial role in distinguishing between safe and threatening situations. When this area is disrupted, as it often is during traumatic experiences, the brain may struggle to differentiate between past trauma and present-day triggers. This can lead to heightened fear responses and difficulty regulating emotions, perpetuating the cycle of trauma-related distress.

In 2022, researchers from a university in Finland reported that the oscillations of the brain, along with functions like respiration and heartbeat, are coupled together. This allows widespread neuronal networks to communicate within both the brain and the body. Some of these brain oscillations, particularly those involving the neocortex, thalamus, and hippocampus, are foundational to the consolidation of memories, especially memories of life events.

The researchers also proposed that beyond the well-known brain oscillations and sharp-wave ripples in the hippocampus during sleep, something else may be happening in the hippocampus to record these memories: a phenomenon called the dentate spike. They believe that during the dentate spike, memories could be modified. Additionally, they suggested that the rhythm of breathing could influence memory consolidation in the hippocampus.

This research aligns with Somatic Therapy principles by emphasizing the interconnectedness of the body rhythms, such as breathing and heartbeat, brain activity, and memory processes. By suggesting that breathing rhythms influence memory consolidation, these findings provide scientific support for Somatic Therapy's use of bodily regulation practices to improve emotional processing and memory integration. This connection underscores how such practices could be particularly effective in addressing trauma-related symptoms and supporting overall therapeutic outcomes.

Neuroplasticity

The brain's ability to reorganize itself by forming new neural connections is called neuroplasticity. It means our brains are not fixed; they can change and heal.

The whole concept of neuroplasticity is one that traces back to the 19th and 20th centuries. Surprisingly, the concept of neuroplasticity wasn't accepted until much later. Scientists originally thought that once someone became an adult, their brain was unchangeable. That is, until it was proposed in the early 1900s that neurons could grow new connections.

In the 1940s, the idea that "cells that fire together, wire together" came forth. This concept led to scientists believing that somehow, learning and experience could shape the brain. By the 1960s to 1980s, there was a lot of backlash amongst scientists who did not want to believe that the adult brain could change. Researchers then started to show evidence in animals and humans that brain injuries, brain damage, or environmental changes could allow the brain to reorganize itself.

From the 1990s on, functional MRI imaging techniques showed brain changes in real time. This is when the concept of neuroplasticity became widely recognized. Scientists ran studies that showed the brain recovered from strokes and trauma and new neurons could grow in certain parts of the brain such as the hippocampus.

Today, neuroplasticity is a foundational concept in psychology, neuroscience, and medicine, assisting people in stroke recovery, dealing with traumas, learning disabilities, and mental health challenges. The brain really is dynamic and capable of adapting across one's entire lifespan.

The Connection of Somatic Therapy and Neuroplasticity

Through Somatic Therapy, we can encourage neuroplasticity by creating new, healthier patterns in response to stress and trauma. This is where science meets the practice. By focusing on body awareness and physical sensations, ST helps us rewire our brains, fostering resilience and emotional stability.

Scientific studies validate the effectiveness of Somatic Therapy. Peter Levine's research on trauma recovery through Somatic Experiencing has shown that animals in the wild, despite facing life-threatening situations, rarely suffer from trauma. He attributed this to their natural ability to discharge the energy associated with traumatic events through physical movements.

Levine adapted this concept for humans, developing techniques that help us release stored trauma through bodily sensations and movements. Research on Somatic Experiencing has demonstrated its positive impact on PTSD-related symptoms, affective *Movement eliminates the tension and* disorders, and emotional health, though more *stress in animals.* rigorous studies are needed to solidify these findings.

The Polyvagal Theory, introduced by Stephen Porges, offers another layer of understanding. This theory explains how the vagus nerve, a critical part of the autonomic nervous system, regulates our stress responses. The vagus nerve influences our heart rate, digestion, and facial expressions.

Take a look at the diagram of how the vagus nerve is part of the sympathetic and the parasympathetic nervous systems and all the organs that it affects.

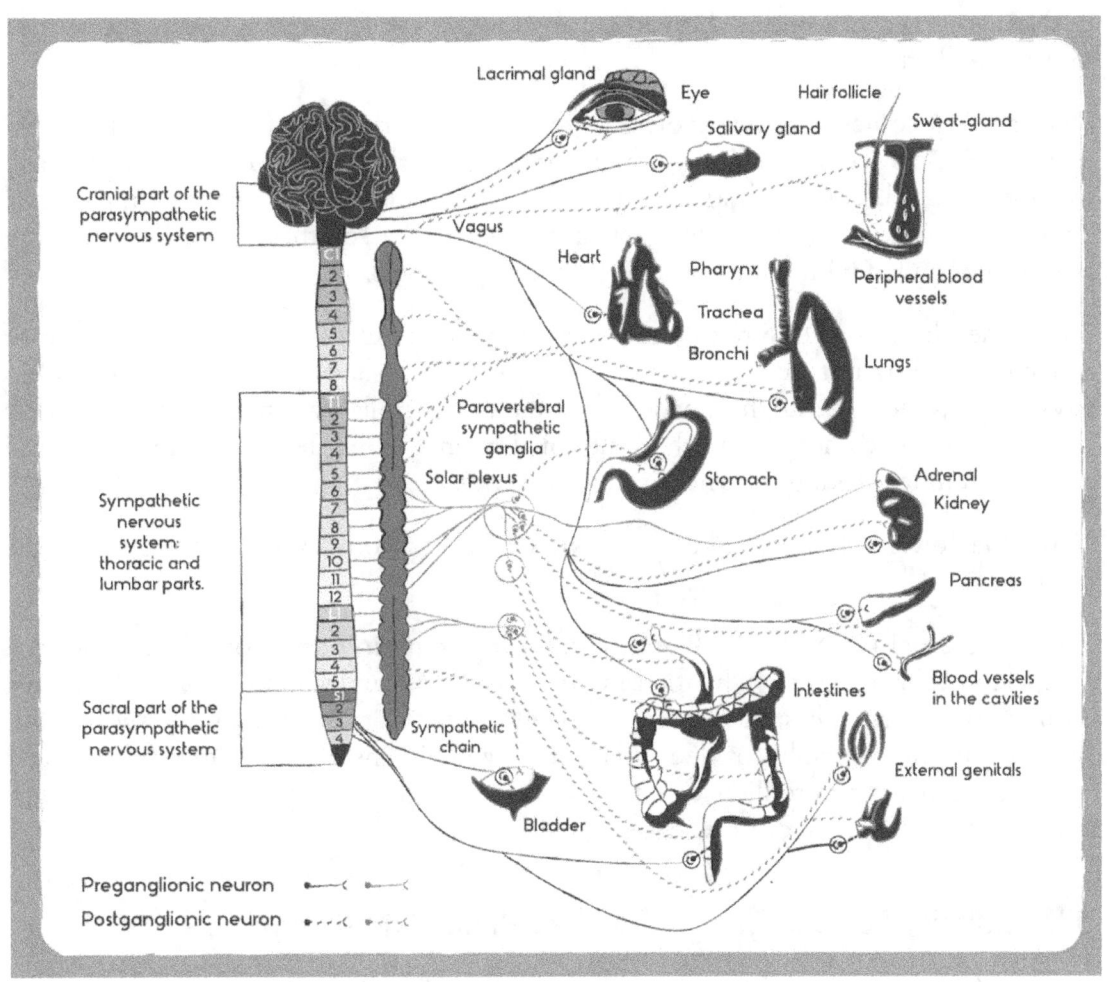

The vagus nerve plays a central role in what Porges calls the "social engagement system," which is essential for feeling safe and connected to others. When we experience trauma, this system can become dysregulated, making it challenging to feel secure or engage socially.

Polyvagal Theory has practical applications in ST, emphasizing techniques that stimulate the vagus nerve to promote calm and social engagement, such as deep breathing and gentle touch.

Scientific studies have found that our bodies store memories of trauma and stress, often referred to as somatic markers. These are physical manifestations of emotional experiences, like shoulder tension, chronic pain, or a clenched jaw. During Somatic Therapy, these markers can be accessed and released.

For example, someone who has experienced a traumatic event might carry tension in their chest. By focusing on this sensation and allowing it to move and change, the individual can begin to release the stored trauma and experience relief. Techniques like

Body Scanning and Mindful Movement effectively identify and work through these somatic markers.

One case that comes to mind involves a woman who had suffered from a traumatic car accident. She constantly felt a tightness in her chest and throat, which traditional therapy had not alleviated. These feelings affected dressing, undressing, movement during normal household chores, and even sleeping. With ST, she focused on these sensations, noticing how they changed with her breath and gentle movements.

Over time, she was able to release the tension, which reduced her physical discomfort. The emotional trauma of the incident had resulted in a fear of getting in her car to go anywhere, as well as fear that made her shake uncontrollably while driving. Somatic Therapy also helped her process this emotional trauma. Now she can get in her car and drive without fear taking over her driving behavior.

This is the power of Somatic Therapy: it works with the body's wisdom to heal from the inside out.

The science behind Somatic Therapy is both fascinating and complex. It offers a compelling explanation for why focusing on our bodies can lead to profound emotional healing. By understanding the neurobiology of trauma, the role of the autonomic nervous system, and the principles of neuroplasticity, we gain insight into how this therapy facilitates recovery and resilience. This knowledge validates the practice and empowers us to use it effectively in our own lives.

Differentiating Somatic Therapy from Traditional Talk Therapy

When I first encountered Somatic Therapy, I couldn't help but compare it to the traditional talk therapy I was familiar with. During talk therapy or psychotherapy, the therapist and I would primarily discuss thoughts, feelings, and experiences, looking for insight to resolve issues. It was a cognitive process that focused on the mind's role in well-being.

Somatic Therapy, on the other hand, starts with the body. It emphasizes physical sensations and body awareness, aiming to address the root of trauma and stress stored in our bodies. This fundamental difference sets Somatic Therapy apart, offering a unique dimension to healing.

For example, in this photo of a woman getting psychiatric help, if the therapist was a Somatic Therapist, he would be asking questions about what she felt about her body attempting to protect her chest and the front of her body. This question could uncover the deeper emotions she was holding onto.

Somatic therapists are able to break through the type of emotional guarding seen in this client.

In talk therapy, the process often involves exploring past experiences, analyzing thoughts, and discussing emotions. While this can be incredibly beneficial, it sometimes overlooks the physical manifestations of those experiences.

Somatic Therapy, however, integrates body awareness exercises, grounding you in the present moment. This approach helps you become more attuned to physical sensations, such as chest tightness or shoulder tension. By focusing on these sensations, you can uncover and release the underlying emotional issues they represent. It's a holistic method that considers both the mind and body together at the same time, potentially fostering a deeper level of healing.

Advantages of Somatic Therapy

One of the significant advantages of Somatic Therapy that practitioners have discovered is its effectiveness in treating trauma and chronic stress. Trauma often leaves a lasting imprint on the body, manifesting as chronic pain, muscle tension, or other physical symptoms. Imagine how over time, say 40 or 50 years, these alterations in muscle tension could show a direct toll on the body posture. This could be the cause of many age-related changes that do not have to manifest themselves and make us look and feel old.

Somatic Therapy addresses these physical manifestations directly, helping you release stored trauma and find relief. It's particularly beneficial for conditions where traditional talk therapy may fall short.

For instance, someone dealing with chronic stress might find that talking about their feelings doesn't alleviate the physical symptoms. By focusing on Body Awareness, Somatic Therapy offers a more comprehensive approach to managing and reducing stress.

One example of this is the case of a man who had survived a violent assault. Despite years of talk therapy, he continued to experience panic attacks and severe anxiety. It wasn't until he began ST that he found significant relief. By learning to tune into his body's sensations, he could identify the physical triggers of his anxiety and work through them. After identifying them, he could decide whether or not to let them go.

The integration of body awareness exercises helped him process the trauma on a deeper level, reducing the frequency and intensity of his panic attacks. His progress continued to get better and better. This case illustrates how Somatic Therapy can complement and enhance the healing process, especially for trauma survivors.

Another example is the case of a woman who switched from talk therapy to Somatic Therapy to address her chronic stress. In talk therapy, she explored her feelings and thoughts extensively but still felt physically drained and tense. Somatic Therapy introduced her to grounding exercises and mindful movement, which helped her connect with her body and release the tension she had been carrying. Over a few months, she noticed a significant improvement in her general wellness, demonstrating the profound impact of including body-focused practices into her healing.

Despite its benefits, Somatic Therapy is often misunderstood. A common misconception is that it's only about physical exercise. While physical movement and body awareness are crucial, Somatic Therapy involves emotional processing and mindfulness.

Somatic Therapy is not just about moving your body; it's about understanding the connections between your physical sensations and emotional states. During the process, what happens is that you make the connection between your body and your feelings and decide whether or not you want to continue "feeding" this connection. If the answer is no, your body cuts off the connection and your brain stops making neural connections as well.

Somatic Therapy works well for those who haven't experienced severe trauma too. In reality, it benefits anyone looking to enhance their mind-body connection, manage stress, and improve their general health. Consider the idea that Somatic Therapy is for whoever doesn't want to live in their older years, dragging along all the traumas of their life with them each remaining day.

In conclusion, Somatic Therapy offers a distinct and valuable approach to healing, focusing on the body's role in storing and releasing trauma. Integrating Body Awareness exercises and emphasizing the present moment provides a holistic method that can be particularly effective for conditions like trauma and chronic stress. Through real-life case examples, we see the transformative power of Somatic Therapy, dispelling common misconceptions and highlighting its depth and scope.

The Benefits of Somatic Therapy for Trauma and Stress

Managing stress can feel like an uphill battle, especially when every aspect of life seems to be demanding our attention. Somatic Therapy offers practical tools to help manage and reduce this stress by regulating the nervous system. Grounding exercises are a cornerstone of this approach. These exercises anchor you to the present moment, helping to calm the body and soothe the mind.

Grounding exercises may be explained as techniques that bring your awareness back to the present moment, especially when you are feeling overwhelmed, anxious, or disconnected. These exercises anchor you to the here and now by focusing on your body and senses, which calms your nervous system.

<u>Here's an example of how to do a Grounding exercise commonly used in ST:</u>

1. Focus on the sensation of your feet on the ground for a few minutes.

2. Feel the stability and support beneath you.

3. Stay in the moment for at least 30 seconds.

This simple practice can create a profound sense of calm, making the chaos of daily life more manageable.

In the photo below, you can see that when someone is experiencing trauma, they will react in one of five different ways. Fight, flight, or freeze are the most common but fawn and flop are also possible coping mechanisms.

Once a trauma confronts us, we have choices. We may run (flight), fight, stop dead in our tracks (freeze), go limp or lose control (flop), or give in to what is happening (fawn).

Breathwork is another powerful technique for immediate stress relief. It's also considered a grounding exercise.

Breathing exercises involve taking slow, deep breaths that activate the parasympathetic nervous system. This helps counteract the fight-or-flight response.

Think about the last time you felt overwhelmed. Did you notice your breath becoming shallow and rapid?

By consciously slowing your breath, you can signal to your body that it's safe to relax.

Techniques like Diaphragmatic Breathing, where you fill your body with air at the level of your belly rather than your chest, can be incredibly effective at immediately relieving stress.

Over time, these Grounding exercises and somatic practices not only help in the moment but also contribute to long-term stress management by creating new, healthier response patterns.

Rebuilding resilience is another significant benefit of Somatic Therapy. Life inevitably throws challenges our way, and resilience is what helps us bounce back. Somatic Therapy enhances recovery by building awareness of bodily sensations.

In Diaphragmatic breathing, the best way to learn is to feel the motion of your belly. It should expand outward when you breathe in because the breath fills up this area of your body. Many people notice that their belly contracts inward instead of outward. This is called reverse breathing, and must be corrected in order for you to experience calmness in your daily life.

Developing Self-Regulation Skills is the Key to Health

When you learn to tune into your body, you can better understand and manage your stress responses. This awareness is the first step in developing self-regulation skills, which are crucial for handling future stress and trauma. By practicing techniques like Body Scanning and Mindful Movement, you can strengthen your mind-body connection, making you more adaptable and resilient in the face of adversity.

Cultivating inner peace may sound like a lofty goal, but Somatic Therapy makes it accessible through mindful body practices. Guided meditations that focus on bodily sensations, sometimes called Mindfulness exercises, can enhance body awareness and promote a sense of tranquility. These practices encourage you to be fully present in your body, helping you to cultivate self-compassion.

When you approach your body with kindness and curiosity, you create a nurturing environment for healing. Over time, these practices can lead to long-term benefits for mental health, including reduced anxiety and increased emotional stability. Many people have found significant improvements even within the first month of practice.

Enhancing the mind-body connection is the most profound benefit of Somatic Therapy. This connection is the foundation of comprehensive health. When attuned to your body, you can better understand its signals and respond to its needs.

This awareness is not just for therapy sessions; it's something you can integrate into your daily life. Simple techniques like taking a few moments to stretch and notice how your body feels or practicing mindful eating by savoring each bite can strengthen this connection.

I recall a friend who started using these exercises in her daily routine. She would take short breaks throughout the day to stretch gently and focus on her breath. Over time, she noticed a significant improvement in her stress levels and general health. Her experience is a testament to the power of integrating somatic practices into everyday life.

Summary

Somatic Therapy offers many benefits for managing and reducing stress, strengthening coping skills, cultivating inner peace, and enhancing the mind-body connection. Including these practices into your daily routine can create a foundation for long-term well-being and emotional stability. The techniques you will learn in this book are not just for moments of crisis but are tools for everyday life, helping you navigate the ups and downs with greater ease and grace.

Let's continue exploring these transformative practices and see how they can become a part of your life.

Chapter 2

RECONNECTING WITH
YOUR BODY

Listen to your body, it knows more than you think.

—— UNKNOWN

IN MY SOMATIC THERAPY journey, the first time I was instructed to scan my body and notice how the different areas of my body were feeling brought a hefty dose of skepticism along with curiosity. This idea was a new concept for me and quite tricky in the beginning. This practice sounded almost too simple to be effective. Yet, it turned out to be one of the most transformative experiences of my life.

The first time I did a body scan, I noticed sensations in my body that I had ignored for years.

For example, the tightness in my chest that was ever present, and the clenching of my jaws. Why had I not felt them for so long? After pondering this, I concluded that I had just taken them as a fact of life that I would have to live with. I never realized that there were things that could be done to alleviate the physical symptoms themselves and reduce the impact they were having in my life.

Now, it was as if I had found a way to tune into a hidden language my body was speaking. In this chapter, I want to help you discover that same language and connect with your body in a meaningful way.

The Body Scan: A Path to Awareness

Body Scanning is a foundational practice in Somatic Therapy. It involves paying close attention to different parts of your body, one at a time, to notice any sensations you might feel. The purpose is to increase body awareness, which is knowing what is happening in your head, neck, arms, hips, and every part of your body at any point in time.

High body awareness can help you manage stress, reduce tension, and improve all around wellness. Regularly practicing body scans daily can make you more attuned to the signals your body sends, allowing you to respond to stress and emotions more effectively. It's like checking in with an old friend to see how they're doing; only this friend is your body.

Athletes have high body awareness. While they are performing their sport, they are considering how their body is moving. Is there any joint that feels a little locked? Is there any inflammation in any part of their body? Is their spine moving as it should or are there areas that seem locked? Are their muscles feeling strong or is there a muscle or two that are considerably weaker today? These are the kinds of things that are included in body awareness.

Athletes use this high body awareness many times during the day, such as when they wake up, when they are stretching or warming up, and after athletic events as well. If they have had an injury, they will constantly monitor the healing of those tissues and make changes appropriate to their rate of healing.

The Body Scan Process

To start a body scan, follow these different steps:

1. Find a quiet, comfortable space where you won't be disturbed. You can lie down or sit in a comfy chair.

2. Close your eyes and take a few deep breaths to settle into the moment.

3. Begin by focusing on the top of your head. Notice any sensations there, whether it's a feeling of tension, warmth, or even numbness.

4. Slowly move your attention down to your forehead, eyes, and cheeks, observing feelings or sensations without judgment.

5. Continue this process, moving down through your neck, shoulders, arms, and hands, paying attention to each area in turn.

6. As you do this, try to breathe into any areas of tension, imagining the breath flowing into those spots and helping them relax.

7. Next, shift your focus to your chest and abdomen, noticing the rise and fall of your breath.

8. Move down to your lower back and hips, then through your legs, knees, and feet.

9. Take mental note of any area that needs further self-care.

The key is to take your time and really notice what's happening in each part of your body. This practice helps you build a deeper connection with your physical self, making the recognition and release of stored tension and stress easier. Don't be discouraged if in the beginning you find this difficult. I certainly did. I had to really work at being able to isolate how I was feeling in the different areas of my body. With practice, this has become easier for me, and it will for you as well.

There are different variations of body scanning to suit various needs and preferences. If you're short on time, incorporate a quick 5-minute Body Scan into your daily routine. This involves a brief check-in with your body, scanning from head to toe, and noticing any significant sensations.

For a more thorough relaxation experience, consider a deep 30-minute body scan. This allows you to spend more time on each part of your body, providing a more comprehensive sense of relaxation and awareness.

You can also use Guided Body Scans with audio or video support, which can be particularly helpful if you're new to the practice. A quick search on YouTube for "guided body scans" results in many guided meditations to follow.

Integrating body scanning into your daily routine can significantly enhance your ability to manage stress and improve your physical and mental health.

One way to do this is by making it part of your morning routine. Spend a few minutes scanning your body before you start your day. This can help you feel grounded and present. Another option is to integrate body scans before bedtime. This can promote relaxation and improve sleep quality. You can also practice body scans during breaks at work. Taking a few minutes to check in with your body can help reduce stress and increase focus and productivity.

Body Scanning Tip

One practical tip for starting this process of body scanning is to set reminders for yourself to practice the technique. You might set reminders on your phone or jot down a note in your planner.

Consistency is key, so try to make it a regular part of your routine. Remember, the goal is to build a deeper connection with your body, so be patient with yourself. Over time, you'll find that these moments of mindfulness become a natural and rewarding part of your day. As you learn what your body is saying, you will be able to address its reaction to stress early on and not allow time for it to build up and begin to affect other areas of your life.

Adding these practices into your daily life can help you easily navigate the ups and downs that any day may bring. Reconnecting with your body through the simple yet powerful practice of body scanning can enhance your mind–body wellness and cultivate a sense of inner peace.

Grounding Exercises: Techniques to Feel Stable and Present

Grounding exercises have been a lifeline for me during times of stress and anxiety. I believe they will be excellent for you as well. These exercises are crucial because they help create a sense of stability and safety, which is often missing when we're overwhelmed.

Grounding techniques can reduce anxiety and panic by anchoring you to the present moment, making it easier to manage your emotions. Feeling grounded makes you less likely to be swept away by distressing thoughts or feelings. Instead, you can focus and concentrate better, allowing you to navigate challenges more effectively.

5-4-3-2-1 Method

One of the most straightforward grounding techniques is the 5-4-3-2-1 Method. This exercise helps you focus on your surroundings and distract yourself from distressing thoughts.

Here's how to do it:

1. Start by noticing five things you can see around you.

2. Identify four things you can touch, paying attention to their texture and temperature.

3. Then, listen for three sounds, no matter how subtle. This could be traffic noise outside your home, birds chirping in your yard, your refrigerator running, the TV/radio in the background, or office chatter if you are at work while doing this exercise. You are listening for other things going on around you. This takes the focus off of the stressful situation that was causing anxiety.

4. Next, find two things you can smell. Smell them.

5. Lastly, focus on one thing you can taste. Taste it.

This method engages all your senses, helping you stay present and grounded in the moment. It is helpful for people experiencing anxiety, PTSD, panic attacks, and other stress-related disorders. By focusing on other things around you using your 5 senses, you can tame your thoughts and rationally address the trigger/stress-inducing events you are experiencing.

For example, let's say you can hear birds chirping outside. Begin to think about how they are taken care of every day as they live in nature, raise their babies, get ready to migrate, etc. These thoughts can replace the negative loop going through your mind continually during stressful situations.

Touch Method

There are many ways to do Grounding techniques. Some will give you general benefits while others will give you benefits when you are in a stressful situation. Throughout this book, you will read exercises that have been previously discussed; however, they are included again because they can be used to address another benefit.

Another simple yet effective grounding technique involves using touch.

Follow this simple procedure:

1. Find an object that is close to you—a smooth stone, a textured piece of fabric, or even a piece of jewelry—and hold it in your hand.

2. Focus on its texture, weight, and temperature for a few minutes.

This tactile focus can be incredibly soothing and helps divert your mind from anxious thoughts.

Grounding Through Movement Method

Similarly, Grounding through Movement can also be beneficial. Simple actions like walking or stretching can reconnect you with your body and the present moment.

Here's the method:

1. As you walk, pay attention to the sensation of your feet hitting the ground. This can be especially beneficial when walking in nature.

2. Notice the scents around you and the sound of the breeze in the trees. Listen for the chatter of birds nearby and develop a grateful appreciation for the beauty of the world around you.

3. If stretching, notice how your muscles feel as they lengthen and relax.

Add Visualization and Breathwork to What You Know

Once you become more comfortable with basic grounding exercises, you can take them to the next level. There are a lot more advanced practices to explore. Visualization techniques can be particularly powerful.

Here's one Visualization exercise that I always return to:

1. While standing, imagine roots growing from your feet into the ground.

2. Visualize these roots anchoring you and providing stability and support.

3. In return, I visualize the earth giving back to me energy and sustenance and filling me with wisdom. I am sure you have heard Earth referred to as "Mother Earth." This is very appropriate because what a mother provides is nourishment, support, and wisdom.

Nature Grounding Technique

Another effective approach is using Nature Grounding. Walking barefoot on grass or soil can help you feel more connected to your environment and yourself. The natural textures and sensations underfoot can be incredibly grounding and calming. Plus, negative ions from the earth come up into the ion channels in your feet, which then act as antioxidants in your body.

Here's the procedure:

1. Remove your shoes and socks and place them on the grass or nearby soil. You can sit in a chair while doing this or stand. If standing, you can walk in the grass for 10 to 20 minutes.

2. You may also sit or lie down directly on the grass for the same amount of time.

3. Put your shoes and socks back on and continue your daily activities.

Grounding in this manner has become a popular trend; however, there are some additional details that you should know.

1. If you have electrical wires underground, do not do Nature Grounding in this area. Some towns do not have any electric wires above the ground that connect to homes. The electrical charge from wires underground may be filled with dirty electricity, which is harmful to the body.

2. Some people use grounding mats or grounding mattress covers to lie on during the day or night. These may be good, but they need to be plugged into grounded outlets in the home. When doing this, remember that you should not plug them into outlets that are associated with a home found to have dirty electricity or electrical problems.

3. If you do have dirty electricity in your home, you must plug the grounding mat or mattress into the ground outside (but not in the ground where there are buried electrical wires).

Here's an example of how this may play out so you understand it more fully. Louise was exposed to excessive radiation from an internet router that put out 100 times the normal radiation that was allowed by the government for several months without knowing it. It ended up destroying her health, bringing her heart's ventricular function to only one-third of its normal capacity.

She had an EMF specialist and Radiation Specialist come to her home to ensure the situation was remedied. The house she was renting had dirty electricity, which was remedied by cutting off the breaker to her bedroom at night. Dirty electricity is unwanted electrical energy that travels through your wiring, causing interruptions and irregularities in the flow of electricity, like surges or spikes. It's like static on a radio but in your home's electrical system.

A few years later, she decided to get a grounding mattress cover. A friend plugged the mattress cover into the outlet and a few days later, she found it nearly impossible to get out of bed in the morning. After a while, she and her friend determined that even though the electricity was still turned off at night in her bedroom, the dirty electricity was still circulating and was going through the cording of the grounding mattress cover. She was fine once they connected the cording to a ground stake that went outside to her backyard. There were no underground electrical wires in her backyard.

Combining Grounding with Breathwork

Combining breathwork with Grounding exercises can enhance their effectiveness.

Here's a way to do that.

1. As you practice deep breathing, focus on the sensation of your feet on the ground.

2. Feel the support beneath you with each inhalation and exhalation.

3. Pay attention to the physical support you are feeling and the energetic support that our wonderful earth has to share. Fill your heart with gratitude for the wisdom of the planet's design and how it has provided so much to every living soul over the millennium.

This combination can help you stay present and calm, making it easier to manage stress and anxiety.

Additional Tips on General Grounding Exercises

Grounding exercises can be seamlessly integrated into other somatic practices for added benefits. Grounding can help you feel more stable and present before and after Body Scans, enhancing the overall effectiveness of the session.

Here are some additional tips:

1. During moments of emotional distress, start grounding. Look for immediate relief. When you regain a sense of control, you will know you are done.

2. Introduce grounding into your daily mindfulness routines. For instance, starting your day with a grounding exercise can set a positive tone, while ending the day with one can promote relaxation and better sleep.

3. Set reminders for yourself. When I first started practicing grounding exercises, I found setting daily reminders helpful. A simple note on my phone or a sticky note on my desk would prompt me to take a moment to ground myself. Over time, these practices became second nature, providing a reliable way to manage stress and stay connected to the present moment. Two helpful sites are www.earthing.com and www.ultimatelongevity.com

The beauty of Grounding exercises lies in their simplicity and versatility. You can always find a moment to ground yourself at home, work, or out in nature. These practices are not about escaping reality but about finding stability within it. By adding Grounding exercises into your daily routine, you can create a foundation of calm and resilience that supports you through life's ups and downs.

Pendulation: Swinging Between States for Resilience

Pendulation involves moving between states of calm and distress, like a pendulum swinging back and forth. The idea is not to avoid discomfort but to learn how to navigate between these states smoothly. This movement helps you build emotional regulation and resilience, allowing you to handle life's ups and downs more effectively.

By practicing Pendulation, you can experience distress without becoming overwhelmed and find your way back to a sense of safety and calm. Imagine what it would be like when you walk into a situation full of stress and then can easily 'walk out' of it as if you were walking out of a room. This is the potential advantage of using Pendulation.

To practice pendulation, follow these steps:

1. Start by focusing on a part of your body that feels safe and relaxed. It could be as simple as noticing the gentle rise and fall of your breath or the feeling of your feet resting on the ground.

2. Allow yourself to fully experience this sense of calm.

3. Once you feel anchored, gently direct your attention to an area of your body that feels tense or uncomfortable.

4. Notice the sensations there without trying to change them. This might feel challenging, but remember, the goal is to observe, not to fix.

5. After a few moments, shift your focus back to the relaxed area, allowing yourself to return to that sense of safety. This back-and-forth movement helps your nervous system learn to regulate itself, building resilience over time.

6. Realizing that you can control your emotions rather than let them control you is a huge step toward growth and progress. Learning to master your emotions is very empowering, and as you become proficient in this, your confidence in any situation will be evident.

Is Pendulation Safe for Those with Anxiety?

Pendulation is incredibly useful in daily life. During stress or anxiety, you can use this technique to manage your emotional state.

For example, here are the steps to do exactly that:

1. If feeling overwhelmed at work, take a moment to focus on your breath or a part of your body that feels calm.

2. Gently acknowledge the tension in your shoulders or chest before returning your focus to the calm area. This can help you regain a sense of control and composure.

Pendulation is also valuable in therapeutic settings, where a professional guide can help you navigate between states of distress and safety. It's an effective way to process trauma without becoming overwhelmed, allowing for gradual healing. Additionally, adding Pendulation into a regular self-care routine can enhance overall resilience, making it easier to handle everyday stressors.

Combine Pendulation with Other Methods

Combining Pendulation with other somatic practices can amplify its benefits.

Here's a way to do that:

1. Use breathwork alongside pendulation. This can deepen your sense of calm and help you move through discomfort more smoothly.

2. As you focus on your breath, allow it to guide you between states of relaxation and tension. This can enhance your ability to stay present and grounded, even during challenging moments.

3. Grounding exercises can also complement Pendulation. Before you begin, take a moment to ground yourself by noticing the sensation of your feet on the floor or holding an object with a reassuring texture. This can provide a stable foundation, making navigating between states of calm and distress easier.

Integrating Pendulation into Mindfulness and Meditation practices can further enhance your emotional well-being. As you meditate, practice moving your focus between areas of calm and tension, observing the sensations without judgment. This can help you cultivate a more profound awareness and acceptance, fostering emotional balance.

I'm Uncomfortable—What Do I Do?

Remember that it is okay to initially feel discomfort when you try these new techniques. You only feel discomfort because they are new to you. By allowing yourself to move between states of calm and distress, you will learn to handle difficult emotions without being consumed by them.

This realization is empowering and will help in your healing process. Pendulation teaches you that there are ways to navigate discomfort with grace and compassion. This technique has become an invaluable part of my self-care routine. Like everyone else, my day often reveals stressful situations I am facing, but with Pendulation, I know that the stress felt in these situations will be overcome within minutes afterward.

This technique has released a lot of anxiety from the past that I didn't know I was carrying. The minute I perceived a stressful situation was on the horizon, I noticed agitation in my mind and body about it. This agitation continued until the stressful situation was experienced, and I noticed it affected how I interacted with others during the situation.

With Pendulation, I don't go into stressful situations with preconceived notions that they will be difficult. Instead, I find myself simply dealing with them and returning to life as usual afterward. I am sure that Pendulation will bring you distinct benefits as well.

Pendulation is Natural Stretching and Body Awareness

Pendulation might sound like a fancy term, but you've likely done it without even realizing it. Have you ever seen a cat stretch after waking up? That's Pendulation.

In Somatic Therapy, Stretching Pendulation is a mindful stretching technique that helps you reconnect with your body and release tension. Pendulation is about natural, organic movement, unlike traditional stretching, which can sometimes push your muscles too far. It involves a contracting, releasing, and resting sequence, allowing your muscles to reset their length and tension. This natural stretching is crucial for increasing body awareness, enhancing flexibility, and promoting well-being.

To practice stretching pendulation, follow this procedure:

1. Start by noticing the natural stretches your body wants to make, especially when you first wake up. These are often spontaneous and feel good, like a yawn paired with a full-body stretch.

2. Pay attention to these movements and see if you can enhance them by adding more awareness.

3. As you stretch, focus on the sensations in your muscles. Feel the gentle pull and the release that follows. This mindful approach turns a simple stretch into a powerful tool for body awareness and tension release.

4. Next, try mixing in slow, mindful stretches into your routine. For instance, as you stretch your arms above your head, move slowly and with intention.

5. Notice the sensations in your shoulders, arms, and back.

6. Breathe deeply, coordinating your movements with your breath.

7. Inhale as you stretch, feeling your muscles lengthen, and exhale as you release the stretch, allowing your body to relax.

This combination of movement and breath enhances the stretch and helps calm your nervous system.

How is Pendulation Beneficial?

Adding Pendulation into your daily life can be incredibly beneficial. A morning Pendulation practice can set a positive tone for the day.

When you wake up, take a few moments to stretch mindfully before getting out of bed. This can help you start the day feeling more connected to your body. During the day, take short breaks to stretch and reset. Even a few minutes of mindful stretching can help reduce tension and increase focus. Before bedtime, gentle stretches can help you unwind and prepare for a restful sleep.

By making Pendulation a regular part of your routine, you can maintain flexibility, release tension, and stay connected to your body.

Mix Pendulation with Other Exercises

Pendulation can be seamlessly integrated with other somatic and Mindfulness practices. For instance, you can use Pendulation with Body Scans. After scanning your body and noticing areas of tension, use mindful stretches to release that tension.

Combining Pendulation with Grounding exercises can enhance the sense of stability and presence. For example, imagine roots growing from your feet into the ground as you stretch, anchoring you firmly. This imagery can deepen the grounding effect.

Integrating Pendulation into other movement routines can also be beneficial. For those of you who do yoga, focus on the sensations of each stretch and move mindfully, coordinating your movements with your breath. This can enhance the overall effectiveness of your practice and help you stay present.

Summary

Pendulation is about listening to your body and responding with kindness. It's a way to honor your body's needs and connect deeply with yourself. By bringing Pendulation into your daily routine, you can build a foundation of body awareness that supports your physical, mental, and spiritual well-being. So, the next time you feel the urge to stretch, take a moment to do it mindfully. Feel the sensations, breathe deeply, and enjoy the sense of release and relaxation that follows.

As you continue to explore Somatic Therapy, you'll find that these simple yet powerful techniques can help you navigate life's challenges with greater ease and grace.

In the next chapter, we'll delve deeper into practical exercises for daily practice, offering more tools to support your healing and growth.

Below are a few charts that summarize the benefits of the somatic exercises in this chapter.

Exercise	Ease of Practice	Time Commitment
Body Scan (Regular, 5-Minute, 30-Minute)	Easy	Quick (5 mins)
5-4-3-2-1 Method	Easy	Quick (5 mins)
Touch Method	Easy	Quick (5 mins)
Grounding Through Movement	Moderate	Moderate (5–10 mins)
Visualization	Moderate	Moderate (5–10 mins)
Nature Grounding	Moderate	Moderate (5–10 mins)
Pendulation (General)	Moderate	Moderate (5–10 mins)
Stretching Pendulation	Easy	Quick (5 mins)

Exercise	Relaxation	Manage Stress	Instant Calm	Regulates Emotions	Better Sleep	Clear Mind
Body Scan (Regular, 5-Minute, 30-Minute)	✓	✓	✓	✓	✓	✓
5-4-3-2-1 Method	✓	✓	✓	✓		✓
Touch Method	✓	✓		✓		✓
Grounding Through Movement	✓	✓		✓		✓
Visualization	✓	✓	✓	✓	✓	✓
Nature Grounding	✓	✓		✓	✓	✓
Pendulation (General)	✓	✓	✓	✓		✓
Stretching Pendulation	✓	✓		✓	✓	✓

Chapter 3

Exercises for Daily Practice

The body remembers what the mind forgets.

—*Jacob Levy Moreno*

One morning, I was in the middle of a chaotic day, feeling overwhelmed and anxious. My mind was racing, and my heart felt like it was pounding out of my chest. I remembered the breathing exercises I had been doing in my meditation class, so I sat for a few minutes taking deep slow breaths.

Almost instantly, I felt a wave of calm wash over me. That simple act of focusing on my breath became a lifeline, not just for that moment but for many others that followed. This chapter is dedicated to sharing Breathwork techniques like this that can bring instant calm and clarity to your life, just as they have to mine.

Breathwork Techniques for Instant Calm

The importance of Breathwork in managing stress and anxiety cannot be overstated. Our breath is directly connected to our nervous system, bridging our mind and body. When we are stressed, our breathing becomes shallow and rapid, signaling our body to stay in a heightened state of alert.

However, by consciously slowing down our breath, we can activate the parasympathetic nervous system, which promotes relaxation and calm. Breathwork helps regulate our emotions, bringing mental clarity and a sense of control during stressful times.

Diaphragmatic Breathing

One of the most effective basic breathwork techniques is Diaphragmatic Breathing, also known as deep belly breathing.

To practice this:

1. Find a comfortable seated or lying position.

2. Place one hand on your chest and the other on your abdomen.

3. Take a slow, deep breath through your nose, allowing your abdomen to expand while keeping your chest relatively still.

4. Exhale slowly through your mouth, feeling your abdomen fall.

5. Repeat this process for a few minutes, focusing on the rise and fall of your belly.

This technique helps you engage your diaphragm, promoting deeper and more efficient breaths.

Box Breathing

Another simple yet powerful technique is Box Breathing. This method involves inhaling, holding, exhaling, and holding again, each for four counts. This approach is much like Diaphragmatic Breathing, but it involves following a specific count for each breath. You can adjust the duration to be longer or shorter, depending on what feels most beneficial for you. The structured pattern of inhaling, holding, exhaling, and holding again requires attention and presence. This focus helps anchor your mind, reduce distractions, and promote clarity. Box breathing also activates the parasympathetic nervous system, which helps reduce stress and anxiety by lowering cortisol levels and calming the body.

Below is the procedure for doing it.

1. Find a comfortable seated or lying position. If sitting, make sure your back is straight.

2. Place one hand on your chest and the other on your abdomen.

3. Take a slow, deep breath through your nose, allowing your abdomen to expand while keeping your chest relatively still.

4. Exhale slowly through your mouth, feeling your abdomen fall.

5. Inhale through your nose for a count of four.

6. Hold your breath for another count of four.

7. Exhale slowly through your mouth for four counts.

8. Hold your breath again for four counts.

9. Repeat this cycle for several minutes.

Box Breathing can help regulate your breathing rhythm, reduce stress, and improve mental focus.

4-7-8 Breathing Technique

The 4-7-8 Breathing Technique, developed by Dr. Andrew Weil, is another excellent method for calming the mind and body. It is known for promoting relaxation and better sleep. The calming affect it has on anxiety, can also help with emotional regulation.

Here's his procedure:

1. Begin by exhaling completely through your mouth.

2. Close your mouth and inhale quietly through your nose for a count of four. Hold your breath for a count of seven.

3. Exhale completely through your mouth for a count of eight.

4. Repeat this cycle three to four times.

This technique can help lower anxiety and promote better sleep.

Alternate Nostril Breathing

Advanced breathwork techniques offer additional benefits for those ready to deepen their practice. Alternate Nostril Breathing, also known as Nadi Shodhana, balances breath through each nostril, enhancing cardiovascular function and lowering heart rate. This technique balances the left and right brain hemispheres which enhances oxygenation and circulation, which in turn, can reduce fatigue and promote a steady, revitalized energy level.

To practice:

1. Sit comfortably and close your right nostril with your thumb.

2. Inhale deeply through your left nostril, then close it with your ring finger.

3. Open your right nostril and exhale through it.

4. Inhale through your right nostril, close it, and exhale through your left.

5. Continue this pattern for five minutes.

Breath of Fire Technique

Breath of Fire is a more vigorous technique involving rapid, rhythmic breathing. This technique will provide an energy boost and improve your ability to focus. This can also have an immediate stimulating effect on your nervous system. If your breathing is rapid or shallow initially, this exercise will help you feel energized, alert, or even euphoric but it can also lead to feelings of anxiety or agitation if overdone.

With practice, it can lead to a balanced and energized state that ultimately enhances the parasympathetic response over time.

Here's how to get started:

1. Sit comfortably with your spine straight.

2. Take a few deep breaths.

3. Then, start breathing rapidly through your nose, keeping your mouth closed.

4. Focus on quick, forceful exhalations, allowing the inhalations to happen naturally.

5. Continue this for one to three minutes.

This Breath of Fire exercise can increase energy levels and clear the mind.

Coherent or Resonant Breathing

Coherent or Resonant Breathing involves breathing at a rate of five breaths per minute. This practice maximizes heart rate variability and reduces stress.

Here's the procedure:

1. Inhale for a count of five.

2. Exhale for a count of five.

3. Repeat this rhythm for several minutes.

Coherent Breathing can enhance emotional regulation and promote a sense of calm and balance.

Weave Breathwork Into Your Daily Routine

Integrating breathwork into your daily routine is something that many people begin doing early in their healing journey. They create a 'schedule' that fits into their day. An example is below.

Time of Day	Activity
Morning	3 Box Breathing exercises or (about 2 minutes total), 1 set of Coherent Breathing or Breath of Fire Breathing (2 minutes total). End with a few deep, relaxing breaths.
Stressful Situation	Diaphragmatic Breathing till you don't feel stressed.
Before Bed	4-7-8 Technique and/or Alternate Nostril Breathing

Body Awareness Practices: Listening to Your Inner Wisdom

Body Awareness is something many of us overlook, yet it's crucial for our mental and physical health. When you become more in tune with your body, you enhance the mind-body connection, making it easier to recognize and respond to bodily signals. This awareness helps you prevent and manage stress-related symptoms.

Think about the last time you felt stressed. Did your shoulders tense up? Did your stomach churn? These are your body's signals, trying to tell you something. By tuning into these signals, you can address the underlying issues before they become more significant problems.

Progressive Muscle Relaxation

One effective way to increase body awareness is through Progressive Muscle Relaxation. This exercise involves tensing and then relaxing different muscle groups in your body.

Here's how to do it:

1. Start by finding a comfortable position, either sitting or lying down.

2. Begin with your feet, tensing the muscles as tightly as possible for a few seconds, then slowly releasing the tension.

3. Move up to your calves, thighs, and so on until you've worked your way up to your head.

4. The process should take about 20-25 minutes.

This practice helps you become more aware of where you hold tension and teaches you how to release it. Locating and releasing this tension, will bring relaxation, body awareness, reduce stress, improve sleep, and help with feeling grounded.

Sensory Awareness Exercises

Sensory Awareness Exercises are another excellent method for tuning into your body. These exercises focus on sensory inputs like touch, sound, and sight.

For example, you can sit quietly and notice the sounds around you. You can also notice the texture of the chair you're sitting on or the feeling of your clothes against your skin. You can also practice this while eating, savoring the flavors and textures of your food. These exercises ground you in the present moment, reducing stress and enhancing your total wellness.

Mindful Movement

Mindful Movement is another powerful tool for increasing body awareness and reducing stress. It involves moving slowly and paying close attention to your body's sensations.

Here's the method:

1. Try gentle yoga poses or simple stretches.

2. As you move, focus on how your muscles feel, the stretch in your limbs, and the movement of your joints.

This practice increases your body awareness and helps you develop a more mindful approach to physical activity. It also helps with flexibility and emotional regulation and connecting to the present moment.

Mindful Eating

Mindful Eating is another daily practice that can enhance body awareness. Instead of rushing through meals, take the time to savor each bite. Notice the flavors, textures, and how your body responds to the food. This practice not only improves digestion but also makes eating a more enjoyable experience. It can also help manage emotional eating by taking a moment to determine whether you are genuinely hungry or eating in response to stress.

Walking Meditation (or Mindful Walking)

Walking Meditation is another great way to maintain body awareness.

Here's how to do it:

1. As you walk, focus on the sensation of your feet hitting the ground.

2. Notice the movement of your legs and the rhythm of your steps.

This can be done anywhere, whether walking to work, taking a stroll in the park, or moving around your home. Walking Meditation helps you stay grounded and connected to your body, making it easier to manage stress and remain present. When combined with mindful breathing, it activates the parasympathetic nervous system, reducing stress and promoting relaxation.

Tip: How to Stay Aware of Your Body During the Day

To maintain body awareness throughout the day, consider making regular body check-ins. Set a few reminders on your phone to pause and notice any sensations in your body. Are your shoulders tense? Is your jaw clenched? Taking a moment to check in with your body can help you release tension and stay present.

Benefits of Combining Body Awareness with Other Practices

Combining Body Awareness with other practices can amplify its benefits. But what are the benefits?

1. Mindful Stretching routines can help you become more aware of your body while improving flexibility and reducing tension. As you stretch, focus on the sensations in your muscles and joints.

2. Combining them can make your workouts more effective and enjoyable. During exercise, pay attention to how your body feels. Notice your breathing, the movement of your muscles, and any areas of tension.

3. It can also help you manage stress and respond more thoughtfully in social situations. Using body awareness in social interactions is another valuable practice. Notice your physical reactions during conversations. Are you clenching your fists? Is your heart rate increasing? Awareness of these signals gives you the edge in social situations, helping you look calm and approachable.

4. Combining them can enhance your whole body awareness and allow you to recognize and respond to bodily signals more effectively. Doing so fuses body awareness practices into your daily routine and prevents and manages stress-related symptoms.

These practices are simple yet powerful tools that can significantly improve your physical and mental health.

Daily Movement Practices to Release Tension

I've come to deeply appreciate the role of movement in stress relief. Regular movement helps release physical tension and significantly reduces stress.

When you move, your body engages muscles, boosts circulation, and stimulates the release of endorphins, which are natural mood lifters. This movement impacts the nervous system by promoting relaxation and balance. Releasing stored tension through movement alleviates physical discomfort and helps clear mental fog, making it easier to focus and think clearly. Movement is like a reset button, offering a way to shake off the stress accumulating in our muscles and minds throughout the day.

Simple Daily Movement

Simple Daily Movement practices are effective and easy to incorporate into your routine. Gentle stretching is a great place to start. You don't need to be a yoga expert to benefit from basic stretches. Moving daily will improve your mobility and flexibility. Two very important attributes, especially as we age.

Here's how to start:

1. Start by reaching your arms above your head, feeling the stretch through your shoulders and back.

2. Bend slowly to each side, stretching your torso.

3. Then, gently twist your upper body, keeping your hips facing forward.

These movements help release tension in your upper body and improve flexibility.

Joint Rotations

Joint rotations are another simple practice:

1. Rotate your wrists in slow, controlled circles.

2. Then rotate your ankles in slow, controlled circles.

3. Next is your shoulders. Rotate them in slow, controlled circles.

4. Finally, rotate your neck in slow, controlled circles.

This increases mobility and reduces stiffness, making you feel more agile and less tense.

Shake It Out (Shaking Technique)

Sometimes, the best way to release stress and pent-up energy is to shake it out.

Here's how to do it:

1. Stand up and start shaking your arms.

2. Then shake your legs.

3. Then shake your whole body.

4. During the shaking, let go of any stiffness, letting your body move freely. This might feel silly at first, but it's incredibly effective.

Shaking helps release built-up tension and can leave you feeling lighter and more relaxed. You might even find yourself smiling or laughing, adding an extra boost of positivity to your day.

Whole Body Vibration

Another thing I have incorporated lately is the use of a Vibration Plate. In just 10 minutes a day, I have given my body a thorough "shaking" and reached areas that might not be affected by just shaking my arms or legs.

The vibration plate stimulates the lymphatic system to help the health journey further. Vibration Plates are available at varying prices, from a few hundred dollars to a few thousand.

Research on whole-body vibration (WBV) has shown that it can positively impact health, including reducing symptoms of anxiety and depression.

You Need a Movement Routine in Your Life

Having movement in your daily life doesn't have to be a chore. A Morning Movement Routine can set the tone for a positive day.

Here's how to do it:

>   1. Start with gentle stretches when you wake up, loosening any stiffness from sleep.

>   2. Take a few minutes to rotate your joints and shake out any lingering tension.

This wakes up your body and also prepares your mind for the day ahead.

Throughout the day, do it like this:

>   1. Take stretch breaks.

>   2. If you're sitting at a desk, set a timer to remind yourself to stand up and stretch every hour.

>   3. You can do quick stretches and joint rotations to keep your body feeling good.

In the evening, create a routine to unwind. Gentle stretches and shaking can help release the tension accumulated during the day, making relaxation and sleep easier.

Add Movement Practices to Stress Relief Practices

Pairing movement practices with other stress-relief techniques can enhance their benefits. Combining movement with breathwork is a powerful way to deepen relaxation.

There are three ways to do this:

1. As you stretch, focus on your breath, inhaling deeply as you reach and exhaling as you release. This synchronizes your body and mind, amplifying the calming effects.

2. Movement can also serve as a warm-up for body scans. Before you begin a Body Scan, spend a few minutes stretching and shaking out tension. This prepares your body to be more receptive and aware during the scan.

3. Integrating movement into Mindfulness practices can further enhance your well-being. For instance, during a mindful movement session, focus on the sensations in your body as you stretch and move. Notice the stretch in your muscles, the movement of your joints, and the rhythm of your breath. This helps you stay present and fully engaged with your body.

How I Incorporate Movement Practices Daily

I used to suffer from tension headaches and chronic back pain, often exacerbated by stress. Regular stretching, joint rotations, and shaking out my body have helped alleviate these issues. I start my mornings with a short Stretching routine or 10 minutes on the Vibration plate. I also take regular Stretch breaks throughout the day and unwind with Gentle Movement in the evening.

This simple yet effective approach has improved my physical comfort and general wellness. Movement has become a natural part of my day, a tool I can rely on to release tension and reduce stress.

Self-Regulation Tools for Emotional Management

When you understand self-regulation, you can better manage your emotions and stress. Self-regulation refers to the ability to control one's emotional responses. This doesn't mean suppressing your emotions but means managing the intensity and duration of your emotions.

Mental health depends on the skill of effective self-regulation, which helps you navigate life's challenges more easily. Regulating your emotions makes you better equipped to handle stress, reduce anxiety, and maintain emotional stability. This skill is particularly beneficial in high-stress environments, where quick emotional responses can lead to negative outcomes.

Techniques to Develop Self-Regulation

Several practical tools and techniques can help you develop self-regulation. Three of the most commonly used tools are Emotional Labeling, Grounding Exercises, and Visualization Techniques. Grounding and Visualization exercises were mentioned previously but this time, they are included for the distinct purpose of developing this most important skill of self-regulation.

Emotional Labeling

Emotional Labeling involves identifying and naming your emotions as you experience them. For instance, if you feel a sudden rush of anger, take a moment to acknowledge it by saying to yourself, "I am feeling angry." Naming your emotions can create a sense of distance, making managing it easier. Emotional labeling helps you become more aware of your feelings, allowing you to respond thoughtfully rather than impulsively.

Grounding Exercises

Grounding Exercises discussed previously are another effective tool for emotional regulation. These exercises help anchor you to the present moment, making it easier to manage intense emotions.

The steps of a simple grounding technique is below:

1. Focus on the sensation of your feet on the ground.

2. Feel the texture of the floor or the grass beneath you.

3. Notice the weight of your body pressing down.

4. Repeat until you notice a change in your emotions.

Focusing on physical sensations can help calm your mind and reduce emotional overwhelm.

These Grounding exercises can be beneficial during high stress or anxiety, providing immediate relief and a sense of stability.

Visualization Techniques

Visualization Techniques can also play a significant role in self-regulation. Creating a mental safe space is a powerful way to manage emotions.

<u>Here's how to do it:</u>

1. Close your eyes. Imagine a place where you feel completely safe and relaxed. It could be a beach, a forest, or a cozy room.

2. Visualize this space in detail, paying attention to the colors, sounds, and textures. Make the image in your head full of color and as dramatic as you can make it.

3. Monitor your emotions. Have they subsided? If not, repeat the process for a longer time frame.

Whenever you feel overwhelmed, retreat to this mental safe space for a few moments. This visualization can help you regain a sense of calm and control, making it easier to manage your emotions.

Advantages of Starting Your Day with Self-Regulation

Using self-regulation tools in your everyday life can significantly affect your emotional well-being. But how will you do this?

<u>Consider this way:</u>

1. Start your day with a morning self-regulation check-in.

2. Spend a few minutes identifying how you feel.

3. Name any emotions that are present. Once identified, ask yourself probing questions as to why you are feeling that particular emotion at that particular time. Why is it being felt in that particular part of your body? How can you best address it to limit its impact on your day?

This practice sets a positive tone for the day and helps you stay aware of your emotional state. During stressful situations, use self-regulation techniques to stay centered. Whether it's a grounding exercise or emotional labeling, these tools can help you navigate stress more effectively.

In the evening, take time for reflection and emotional regulation. Review your day, acknowledge any challenging emotions, and use Visualization or Grounding exercises to release any lingering tension.

Combine Self-Regulation Practices with Others

Combining self-regulation with other practices can enhance their effectiveness. Here are some tips:

1. Before and after challenging tasks, take a moment to practice self-regulation. This can help you stay calm and focused, improving your performance and reducing stress.

2. Integrate self-regulation with Body Awareness exercises. Pay attention to your emotional state as you practice Progressive Muscle Relaxation or Mindful Movement. Notice any changes in your emotions as you release physical tension. Using self-regulation tools during these exercises can deepen your mind-body harmony and promote mental and physical health.

3. Journaling is another valuable practice that pairs well with self-regulation. After using techniques like Emotional Labeling or Visualization, write about your experience. Reflect on how these practices helped you manage your emotions and what you learned about yourself. How did you feel before starting an exercise, and how did you feel afterward? This combination of self-regulation and Journaling can provide valuable insights and reinforce positive habits.

Adding these self-regulation tools into my daily routine has been transformative. By practicing Emotional Labeling, Grounding exercises, and Visualization techniques, I can honestly say that I've learned to navigate my emotions more effectively. I start each day with a self-regulation check-in. I use Grounding exercises during stressful moments and end the day with Reflection and Emotional Regulation. These practices have helped me stay centered and calm, even in challenging situations.

Summary

Integrating self-regulation tools into daily life can cultivate emotional health and improve general wellness. As you continue exploring the practices in this book, you'll find that these self-regulation tools are potent allies in your journey toward emotional stability. They provide practical, actionable steps to manage stress and enhance mental health.

Here are the summary tables for all the exercises in this chapter:

Exercise	Ease of Practice	Time Commitment
Diaphragmatic Breathing	Easy	5–10 mins
Box Breathing	Easy	5–10 mins
4-7-8 Breathing Technique	Moderate	5 mins
Alternate Nostril Breathing	Moderate	5–10 mins
Breath of Fire Technique	Challenging	1–3 mins
Coherent/Resonant Breathing	Easy	5 mins
Progressive Muscle Relaxation	Moderate	20–25 mins
Sensory Awareness Exercises	Easy	5 mins
Mindful Movement	Easy	5–10 mins
Mindful Eating	Easy	Varies
Walking Meditation	Easy	5–10 mins

Exercise	Relaxation	Manage Stress	Instant Calm	Regulates Emotions	Better Sleep	Clear Mind
Diaphragmatic Breathing	✓	✓	✓	✓	✓	✓
Box Breathing	✓	✓	✓	✓		✓
4-7-8 Breathing Technique	✓	✓	✓	✓	✓	
Alternate Nostril Breathing	✓	✓	✓	✓		
Breath of Fire Technique		✓				✓
Coherent/Resonant Breathing	✓	✓	✓	✓	✓	
Progressive Muscle Relaxation	✓	✓		✓	✓	
Sensory Awareness Exercises	✓	✓	✓	✓		
Mindful Movement	✓	✓		✓		
Mindful Eating	✓	✓		✓		
Walking Meditation	✓	✓	✓	✓		✓

Exercise	Ease of Practice	Time Commitment
Simple Daily Movement	Easy	5–10 mins
Joint Rotations	Easy	5 mins
Shaking (Shake It Out)	Easy	5 mins
Whole Body Vibration	Moderate	10 mins

Exercise	Relaxation	Manage Stress	Instant Calm	Regulates Emotions	Better Sleep	Clear Mind
Simple Daily Movement	✓	✓		✓	✓	✓
Joint Rotations	✓	✓				
Shaking (Shake It Out)	✓	✓	✓			✓
Whole Body Vibration	✓	✓		✓		✓

Exercise	Ease of Practice	Time Commitment
Emotional Labeling	Easy	1–3 mins
Grounding Exercises	Easy	5 mins
Visualization Techniques	Moderate	5–10 mins

Exercise	Relaxation	Manage Stress	Instant Calm	Regulates Emotions	Better Sleep	Clear Mind
Emotional Labeling		✓	✓	✓		✓
Grounding Exercises	✓	✓	✓	✓		✓
Visualization Techniques	✓	✓	✓	✓		✓

In the next chapter, we'll explore understanding and managing emotions, offering more insights and techniques to support your healing and growth.

Chapter 4

UNDERSTANDING AND MANAGING EMOTIONS

*The body is a reflection of the mind. If you feed your mind with
positivity and light, your body will reflect that energy.*

-- ANONYMOUS

IN MY JOURNEY TO understanding how emotions and physical sensations are related, I started noticing that any time I received challenging news or negative feedback at work, I would instantly feel a sensation in my stomach area and even taste changes in my mouth. This was when I realized the power of emotions over our physical state.

This chapter explores how understanding and managing these physical sensations can lead to emotional regulation and balanced well-being.

Identifying Physical Sensations of Emotions

Your emotions are not just abstract feelings that float around in your head; they manifest physically in your body. This connection between mind and body is a critical concept in Somatic Therapy.

The nervous system plays a crucial role in how you experience emotions. When you feel scared, your amygdala—the brain's alarm system—activates, triggering a cascade of physical responses. Your heart rate might spike, your muscles tense, and your breathing becomes shallow. These are your body's way of preparing to face a threat, even if the "threat" is just a stressful email from your boss. You can refer back to the image in Chapter 1 on how this all works.

How Emotions Manifest Themselves

Different emotions manifest in varied physical ways. Anxiety often feels like a tight chest or a knot in your stomach. Anger might manifest as clenched fists or a flushed face. Sadness can bring a heavy feeling in your limbs and a lump in your throat. Recognizing these physical signs is essential because unacknowledged emotions can have a lasting impact on your health.

Chronic stress, for example, can lead to headaches, high blood pressure and even weaken the immune system. By tuning into these physical sensations, you can address your emotions before they affect your body.

Try using Body Scanning in your routine to better identify these sensations. Set aside a few minutes each day to sit quietly and scan through your body from head to toe. Notice any areas of tension or discomfort and consider what emotions might be causing these sensations.

Journaling can also be a powerful tool. When you experience strong emotions, write down what you feel physically. This practice can help you connect the dots between your emotions and physical sensations.

Mindfulness practices focused on bodily sensations, such as paying attention to your breath or the feeling of your feet on the ground, can also enhance your ability to recognize these signals.

Progressive Muscle Relaxation

One exercise to develop emotional awareness is Progressive Muscle Relaxation with an emotional focus. It's a little different than the previous time it was explained; so pay attention to the details.

Here's how to do it:

1. Lie comfortably on a yoga mat or towel on the floor.

2. Tense your toes. Hold the tenseness for a count of 10.

3. Then relax your toes.

4. Pay attention to any emotional shifts as you do this

5. Continue tensing and relaxing different muscle groups, moving up through your body, such as your foot muscles, calves, quadriceps, buttocks, and more, up to and including your head and face.

6. Then the next time you go through this method, tense the muscles at 50%.

The following time you use this method, tense your muscles to only 25%. Don't forget to release the tension. Progressive Muscle Relaxation allows you to sense tenseness at minute levels. Give yourself about a month to train yourself on this method. It has been found to be very effective.

Progressive Muscle Relaxation can help you become more aware of how emotions influence your physical state. When you are feeling an emotion, it often shows up with muscle tenseness. You may find that talking to your boss creates muscle tension in your back and neck while talking to your neighbor creates facial and neck muscle stress.

But if you can't feel the tenseness, there's a greater likelihood that the emotion can become "stuck" in your body. However, with PMR, your ability to detect very small changes in muscle tension is heightened. This results in you always looking like you can control yourself in a situation of stress, because as soon as you detect it, you release it.

Sensory Tracking

Sensory Tracking is another effective method. Sensory tracking can help promote a deeper connection to your body and its signals. It can also help identify patterns related to stress, triggers, or emotional states. This reduces the likelihood of impulsive responses to stress or discomfort.

For this method, you would:

1. Notice changes in your body temperature, heart rate, or muscle tension throughout the day.

2. Consider what emotions might be causing these changes.

Why You Want To Pay Attention to Physical Sensations

Recognizing the physical sensations of your emotions can significantly improve your emotional intelligence. Intelligence is not just IQ; rather, as Howard Gardner reported in his Theory of Multiple Intelligences, it is composed of different types of intelligence.

He and other prominent scientists reported that these are the ways you can be incredibly smart:

1. Logical-mathematical intelligence

2. Linguistic intelligence

3. Spatial intelligence

4. Musical intelligence

5. Bodily-Kinesthetic intelligence

6. Interpersonal intelligence

7. Intrapersonal intelligence

8. Naturalistic intelligence

9. Existential intelligence

10. Emotional intelligence

11. Creative intelligence

12. Practical intelligence

13. Fluid intelligence

14. Crystallized intelligence

15. Social intelligence

16. Moral intelligence

17. Digital intelligence

18. Spiritual intelligence

Emotional intelligence is the ability to recognize, understand, manage, and influence emotions in yourself and others. It involves self-awareness, self-regulation, motivation, empathy, and social skills. Emotional intelligence overlaps with several other intelligences on the list, such as interpersonal, intrapersonal, existential, creative, social, moral, and spiritual intelligence.

Recognizing how you feel means identifying the physical sensations you are feeling. Surprisingly, many somatic exercise books assume you can identify the physical sensations we all feel. However, many people have to be taught what to look for.

Your physical sensations may include some of the following in the table below.

Emotion	Physical Sensations
Anxiety	Tightness in the chest or throat
	Rapid heartbeat or palpitations
	Shallow breathing or hyperventilation
	Sweaty palms or a queasy stomach
	Restlessness or jittery movements
Anger	Heat rising in the face or ears (blushing)
	Clenched jaw or fists
	Tense shoulders or neck
	A pounding heart or a surge of energy
	Gritting teeth or a feeling of pressure in the head
Sadness	A heavy or sinking feeling in the chest
	Tearfulness
	A lump in the throat
	Slow, shallow breathing
	Low energy or fatigue
	A physical ache, often described as a heartache
Fear	Cold sweats
	Goosebumps
	Tightening of the stomach ("butterflies") or nausea
	Rapid breathing or shortness of breath
	Feeling frozen or paralyzed
	Heightened senses or a sense of hypervigilance

Joy/Happiness	Lightness or warmth in the chest
	Smiling or an uncontrollable urge to laugh
	A sense of expansion or openness in the body
	Increased energy or a spring in your step
	Relaxed muscles and a sense of ease
Love	A warm, fuzzy feeling in the chest
	A calm, steady heartbeat
	A sense of openness and vulnerability
	Relaxation or a gentle tingling sensation
	A desire for physical closeness or connection
Guilt	A churning sensation in the stomach
	Slumped shoulders or avoiding eye contact
	A heavy feeling, particularly in the chest or abdomen
	Sweating or feeling overheated
	A general sense of discomfort or restlessness
Shame	A burning sensation in the face or neck (blushing)
	Looking down or avoiding eye contact
	A tightness in the throat or chest
	Shrinking posture, as if trying to hide
	A sense of weight or pressure in the body
Excitement	Increased energy or jitteriness
	Quickened breathing or a pounding heart
	A tingling sensation in the fingers or toes
	Smiling or laughter that feels uncontrollable
	A feeling of butterflies, similar to nervousness, but with a positive undertone

By becoming more aware of these sensations, you enhance your ability to manage stress and respond to emotional triggers in healthier ways. This heightened self-awareness fosters greater self-compassion as you approach your emotions with curiosity rather than judgment.

For instance, if you notice your chest tightening with anxiety, you can take a moment to breathe deeply and calm your nervous system rather than letting the anxiety spiral out of control. This simple act of acknowledging and addressing your emotions can profoundly impact your physical and mental health. It may help you avoid a trip to the Emergency Room thinking that you are having a heart attack!

Emotional Mapping

Emotional Mapping can also be insightful. This is where you draw or write where you feel different emotions in your body. It's a method that works well for children too. This visual representation can help you understand and manage your emotions better. By pinpointing where you feel certain emotions, you can develop a keen sense of self awareness which can lead to emotional regulation and overall well-being.

Here's the process:

1. Find a quiet place where you feel comfortable.

2. Take a few deep breaths to center yourself.

3. Think about a recent emotional experience.

4. On a piece of paper, draw an outline of a human body.

5. Mark the areas where you felt physical sensations during that emotional experience.

6. Reflect on what these sensations tell you about your emotions.

7. Repeat this exercise with different emotions to build a comprehensive emotional map.

Managing Intense Emotions: Techniques for Self-Regulation

Understanding and managing the physical sensations of your emotions is a decisive step toward emotional regulation. Tuning into your body and recognizing these signals can help you navigate your emotions with greater ease and resilience.

Intense emotions like anger, fear, and sadness can be overwhelming and challenging to manage. You may have noticed that it takes you a long time to "come down" from an anger outburst, or you can't seem to get over the sadness and grief that occurs when a family member dies. Self-Regulation helps cut down the time you stay in these emotional states.

This is important because as you are experiencing these negative emotions, they are also changing your physiology. For example, anger might cause your heart to race and your muscles to tighten, while sadness can lead to a heavy feeling in your chest and a lump in your throat. Anger can be counted on to raise your blood pressure, and sadness may also depress your body functions or affect your appetite.

These intense emotions can be triggered by a range of experiences we are all too familiar with, from relationship conflicts and work stress to traumatic incidents and sudden changes in your environment. It's crucial to address these emotions rather than suppress them. Bottling up intense emotions can lead to long-term physical and mental health issues, including chronic stress and anxiety. The goal is to find effective ways to manage these emotions, so they don't control you.

When You Experience Emotional Shifts, Breathe!

One of the most effective techniques for calming the nervous system during moments of intense emotion is Breathwork. This is why it's one of the most important Somatic Exercises you can learn and why they are being brought up again.

Have you noticed that during moments when you feel overwhelmed, your breath becomes shallow and rapid?

This type of breathing worsens your emotional state. By consciously slowing your breath, you can signal your brain that it's time to relax. Diaphragmatic Breathing, where you take deep breaths into your belly, has been shown to activate the parasympathetic nervous system, promoting a sense of calm and returning your emotional state to normal.

Visualization Techniques are another powerful tool. Creating a mental safe space in your mind's eye can provide immediate emotional relief.

The process is pretty easy:

1. Close your eyes While sitting in a comfortable chair or lying down.

2. Imagine a place where you feel completely safe and relaxed. This could be a beach, a forest, or a cozy room.

3. Picture every detail, from colors to sounds, and allow yourself to fully immerse in this mental sanctuary.

4. Stay there in this imagination for at least a few minutes.

5. Then, return to normal reality.

Grounding Exercises

Grounding Exercises can also be incredibly effective for staying present and centered during intense emotional episodes. The simple grounding technique of focusing on the sensation of your feet touching the ground has been discussed.

Five Senses Method

Here is another simple grounding exercise called the "Five Senses" method.

<u>To do this, look around you for:</u>

- 5 things you can see

- 4 things you can touch

- 3 things you can hear

- 2 things you can smell

- 1 thing you can taste

Doing this process in that order changes your focus and diverts your mind from overwhelming emotions.

Emotional Labeling

Emotional Labeling is another practical technique. This was explained before, but a review may help. When you experience a strong emotion, take a moment to name it. For instance, say to yourself, "I am feeling anxious," or "I am feeling angry." Naming the emotion can create a sense of distance, making it easier to manage.

You may be surprised to find that there are literally hundreds of emotions you may feel. Psychologist Robert Plutchik's research found that although we have eight primary emotions––anger, fear, sadness, joy, disgust, surprise, trust, and anticipation, we can experience over 34,000 unique emotions.

Other psychologists believe that there are 16 human emotions, which can be tracked via facial expressions.

They include:

• amusement	• anger	• awe	• concentration
• confusion	• contempt	• contentment	• desire
• doubt	• elation	• interest	• disappointment
• pain	• sadness	• surprise	• triumph

Review of Adding Self-Regulation Techniques to Your Day

These Self-Regulation techniques added to your daily life can significantly affect how you handle stress and intense emotions. The practice may begin your day with a morning Self-Regulation check-in, spending a few minutes identifying how you feel and Naming

Feelings that are present. This practice sets a positive tone for the day and helps you stay aware of your emotional state.

During stressful situations, use Self-Regulation tools to stay centered. Whether it's a Grounding Exercise or Emotional Labeling, these techniques can help you navigate stress more effectively. In the evening, take time for Reflection and Emotional Regulation. Review your day, acknowledge any challenging emotions, and use Visualization or Grounding exercises to release any lingering tension.

Here's an example day you may have once you start using Self-Regulation techniques:

Time	What Happens	Feeling	Self-Regulation Tool Used
6 am	Dog barking wakes you.	Irritated	Breathwork. Then, address the dog.
7 am	Breakfast burns in pan.	Anger	Emotional labeling
8 am	Rush hour traffic; get cut off, near accident.	Complete overwhelm	Emotional mapping
10 am	Boss piles on new tasks	Unfairness	Visualization of being given justice
Noon	Coffee and lunch spilled everywhere	Mad at self	Diaphragmatic Breathing
2 pm	Phone call from Mom with accusations	Defiance Combative	Grounding exercise
6 pm	Watch the news.	Sadness	Progressive muscle relaxation

Once you really start documenting what happens during the day, you'll start to see that every day is potentially an emotional roller coaster. That's why it's up to you to control your emotions. Imagine that if it takes you two days to come down from the heights of anger and you experience five additional moments of anger in those two days along with sadness, unfairness, disgust, and ten other emotions that each have to be diffused, how well do you think you will do on your own without any tactics?

It's entirely possible that the prisons are full of people who never learned these techniques. The prisoners haven't learned how to release bad feelings, which keep piling up until one day they "snap."

How long should it take you to recover from being rejected by someone you adore? How long does it take you to get back on track after someone tells you your idea is not a good one? How long does it take you to recover when someone bullies you or calls you a bad name? Should you take everything that happens to you personally? What is life like when you can't overcome the daily 'traumas'?

Now think about the long-term benefits of regularly practicing Self-Regulation techniques. They are profound. Enhanced emotional health is one of the most significant benefits. Everyone wants to be surrounded by even-keeled friends who can deal with their emotions. It's an honor for someone to have a friend who reacts to something you did by calmly discussing it or diffusing the situation with laughter.

By learning to navigate intense emotions effectively, you build a stronger emotional foundation, making it easier to bounce back from setbacks. Improved mental health and well-being are also notable benefits, especially with rising mental illness rates. Regular Self-Regulation practices can reduce symptoms of anxiety and depression, leading to a more balanced emotional state.

Better relationships and communication skills are additional long-term benefits. When you can manage your emotions effectively, you're more likely to respond thoughtfully in interactions, leading to healthier and more fulfilling relationships.

Combining these techniques into your daily routine can transform how you experience and manage intense emotions. Whether through Breathwork, Visualization, Grounding Exercises, or Emotional Labeling, these tools offer practical, actionable steps to enhance your emotional strength and well-being.

Co-Regulation: Partner-Based Emotional Support

Co-Regulation is a powerful concept that can transform how you manage emotions through supportive relationships. At its core, co-regulation involves the mutual comforting, supporting, and understanding of emotional and physiological states between two people. It emphasizes the role of social engagement in emotional regulation. This method helps you understand that when you interact with another person, you aren't the only one who has emotions.

When you're emotionally distressed, having someone there to listen, offer comfort, and share your experience can make a difference. This isn't just about feeling good; Co-Regulation has tangible benefits for both partners. It fosters emotional intimacy, builds trust, and enhances resilience, making it easier to navigate life's challenges together. You learn how to back up another person when their emotions need lifting and identify new ways to do the same when someone else lifts you up.

Active Listening and Empathetic Communication

One of the most effective techniques for practicing Co-Regulation is Active Listening and Empathetic Communication. Let's say that your partner is having a terrible day. Do you want to run away and not even deal with it? With Co-Regulation, you stay in the moment and deal with what's happening.

You do it in a way that is active and present. You don't just hear the words your partner is saying. You truly listen to understand their feelings and perspectives. This is best done when you make eye contact, nod, and offer verbal affirmations like "I understand" or "That sounds really tough."

Matching and Mirroring

Reflecting your partner's emotions and body language, known as Matching and Mirroring, can also be incredibly supportive. If your partner is feeling down, the goal is to match your tone to support their emotional state.

For example, if someone just experienced the death of their parent but you just got a raise and are on top of the world emotionally, you wouldn't express that natural exuberance you feel. It would not be taken well by the other person. Instead, you would gently align your posture and tone to create a sense of empathy and connection.

Physical Touch

Physical Touch is another powerful tool. Holding hands, hugging, or even a gentle touch on the arm can provide immediate comfort and reassurance. These small gestures can signal safety and support, helping both partners feel more grounded.

Co-Regulation can take many forms depending on the relationship. It might involve regular emotional check-ins between partners and spouses where you both share your feelings and offer support. For instance, setting aside time each evening to talk about your day can help you both stay connected and emotionally attuned.

Parent-child Co-Regulation can look different but is equally important. For a child, knowing that a parent is there to offer comfort and understanding can be incredibly soothing. The alternative for many children is aloof parents who appear to not care for what's going on in their emotional world. This is not endearing in any way. We all want and need emotional connection to our family members and friends. A lack of it causes people to search for 'love' in all the wrong places.

Simple actions like reading together, holding hands, or even synchronized breathing can help a child feel safe and regulated. In friendships and support groups, Co-Regulation often involves being present for each other during tough times. Whether it's a phone call, a text, or meeting up for coffee, these acts of support can significantly affect emotional well-being.

Building a supportive Co-Regulation practice in your daily life requires intention and consistency. Start by setting aside regular time for emotional check-ins with your partner or loved ones. This could be a weekly date night, a daily debrief after work, or even a quick morning check-in over coffee. Creating a safe and non-judgmental space for sharing emotions is crucial. Make it clear that this is a space where both of you can express your feelings without fear of criticism or judgment.

Consistently practicing Co-Regulation techniques, like Active Listening and Empathetic Communication, can strengthen your emotional bond and enhance mutual support. It's a foundation for good relationships.

<u>How to Do an Emotional Check-In During Your Day</u>

1. Set aside a regular time each day or week for emotional check-ins with your partner.

2. Find a quiet, comfortable space where you won't be interrupted.

3. Take turns sharing your feelings and using "I" statements to express your emotions.

4. Practice active listening, reflecting on what your partner said to ensure understanding.

5. Offer physical comfort, like holding hands or a hug, if appropriate.

6. End the check-in positively, expressing gratitude for each other's support.

Who do you have in your life who is already your Co-regulation partner? For those who live alone, your partner may be your pet! Some pets are very attuned to their owner's emotions. I have a friend who was emotionally numb for most of her childhood and early adult years. It took several pets for her even to realize the importance of expressing emotions in a relationship.

One day, she met a new friend who could read the emotions of pets quite well. This new friend made a statement to her that rocked her world. She said, "Ginger feels your every emotion and responds to it. Did you notice?" She had not noticed at all. Every day was filled with tasks that had to be done, and emotions were never considered. She had grown up in a home where emotions were never acknowledged.

After this day, she began noticing her emotions—and her dog's emotions as well. Although she didn't have any techniques like the ones you are reading about in this book, this was the start of her emotional healing.

I have been blessed with several very close friends and family who are my "Co-Regulation" partners. Their influence in my life has helped me navigate emotional ups and downs with greater ease. They've also strengthened my relationships, creating a deeper sense of trust and intimacy. The beauty of Co-Regulation is that it's a two-way street; as you offer support, you also receive it, fostering a mutual sense of well-being.

Emotional Triggers are Related to Your Boundaries

An emotional trigger is a specific situation, action, or words that elicit a strong emotional response in someone.

For example, let's say that an ex-husband always said the endearing words, "You are my darling…" When you start dating again, you may be out on a date and the new guy says, "That was so great. I feel like I want to call you 'my darling'." As soon as you hear this, you cringe and emotions that were related to your ex-husband flood in. You want to run as fast as possible to escape this new guy. His words were an emotional trigger to your past.

Identifying emotional triggers in yourself and others is an essential step in setting and maintaining boundaries. These reactions often stem from past experiences and can be physical, like a racing heart, or emotional, like sudden anger. If you know what your emotional triggers are, you can deal with them with effective strategies. In a new relationship, you must learn the other person's emotional triggers.

For example, if you've had a negative experience with criticism, a seemingly harmless comment might trigger feelings of inadequacy or defensiveness. Recognizing these triggers is vital because they highlight areas where boundaries must be strengthened. Understanding your triggers helps you anticipate and manage your reactions, allowing you to set limits that protect your emotional well-being.

Likewise, once you know someone else's triggers, you can avoid discussing them in conversations and actions to keep the peace in your relationship. Bringing up someone's emotional triggers will strain and ruin relationships, and you will be perceived as someone who is constantly nagging or demeaning the other person.

Emotional triggers help you set boundaries. Imagine trying to navigate life without any boundaries. It's like driving on a road with no lanes or traffic lights—chaotic and exhausting. Setting healthy boundaries is crucial for emotional well-being. Boundaries are the invisible lines we draw to protect our mental and emotional health. They define what is acceptable and what isn't in our interactions with others.

Healthy boundaries are a buffer, preventing others from overstepping and draining our emotional resources. Without them, we become vulnerable to stress, burnout, and resentment. Poor boundaries can lead to unhealthy relationships, where one person may take advantage of another's kindness or invade their personal space. This imbalance can strain relationships and leave you feeling depleted and unappreciated.

Strategies for Maintaining Good Healthy Boundaries

Practical strategies for setting and maintaining boundaries start with clear and assertive communication.

Here are some useful tips:

1. When expressing your boundaries, use "I" statements to articulate your needs and limits. For instance, you could say, "I need some quiet time after work to recharge," instead of, "You always make so much noise." This approach focuses on your needs without blaming or accusing the other person.

2. Practice self-care and self-respect. Prioritize activities that nurture your well-being and reinforce your self-worth. When you respect yourself, it becomes easier to insist that others do the same.

3. Regularly check in with yourself to ensure your boundaries are respected and adjust them as needed. This ongoing practice helps maintain a balanced and healthy emotional state.

4. Manage your reactions to triggers by having a toolkit of techniques you can rely on in stressful situations. Grounding exercises provide immediate relief by anchoring you to the present moment. Focus on the sensation of your feet on the ground or the texture of an object in your hand. This physical focus can help divert your mind from the emotional storm.

5. Self-soothing techniques, such as Deep Breathing or Grounding, can offer comfort and reduce anxiety.

6. A list of trusted individuals you can turn to for support is also invaluable. Knowing you have someone to talk to, whether it's a friend, family member, or therapist, can make a world of difference when managing emotional triggers.

7. In the bigger picture, setting healthy boundaries and managing emotional triggers are foundational steps in building mental resilience. They enable you to easily navigate life's ups and downs and protect your mental and emotional health.

Summary

As you continue to develop these skills, you'll find that your relationships improve, your stress levels decrease, and your well-being flourishes. By understanding the importance of boundaries and learning to identify and manage your triggers, you're taking proactive steps toward a healthier, more balanced life.

The summary charts are below.

Exercise	Ease of Practice	Time Commitment
Progressive Muscle Relaxation	Moderate	10–20 mins
Sensory Tracking	Easy	5 mins
Emotional Mapping	Moderate	10 mins
Breathwork	Easy	5 mins
Visualization Techniques	Moderate	5–10 mins
Grounding Exercises (Five Senses)	Easy	5 mins
Active Listening	Easy	Varies
Matching and Mirroring	Moderate	5–10 mins
Boundary Management	Moderate	Varies

Exercise	Relaxation	Manage Stress	Instant Calm	Regulates Emotions	Better Sleep	Clear Mind
Progressive Muscle Relaxation	✓	✓	✓	✓	✓	✓
Sensory Tracking	✓	✓		✓		✓
Emotional Mapping	✓	✓	✓	✓		✓

Exercise	Relaxation	Manage Stress	Instant Calm	Regulates Emotions	Better Sleep	Clear Mind
Breathwork	✓	✓	✓	✓	✓	✓
Visualization Techniques	✓	✓	✓	✓		✓
Grounding Exercises (Five Senses)	✓	✓	✓	✓		✓

Exercise	Relaxation	Manage Stress	Instant Calm	Regulates Emotions	Better Sleep	Clear Mind
Active Listening	✓	✓	✓	✓		✓
Matching and Mirroring	✓	✓	✓	✓		✓
Boundary Management		✓	✓	✓		✓

In the next chapter, methods that can be used to heal chronic pain will be discussed. You may be surprised to find out that you do have control over pain. Some of the techniques you have already learned can be "tweaked" to help you control pain.

Chapter 5

HEALING CHRONIC PAIN

The mind and body are not separate.
What affects one, affects the other.

-- ANONYMOUS

CHRONIC PAIN IS AN everyday enemy for so many people, myself included. This chapter addresses alternative approaches to alleviating that pain, rather than relying solely on pain medication or simply resigning oneself to merely having to live with the pain.

Understanding the Mind-Body Pain Connection

Chronic pain is defined as pain that persists for more than three to six months beyond the usual course of an acute illness or injury. It's a condition that affects millions of people, impacting their quality of life and daily functioning.

The nervous system plays a crucial role in pain perception. When you experience an injury, pain signals travel from the affected area to your brain through your nervous system. However, in chronic pain, these signals can become amplified, causing the pain to persist even after the initial injury has healed. This amplification is often influenced by psychological and emotional factors, making the experience of pain both a sensory and emotional phenomenon.

If you don't have chronic pain, think about it like this: Let's say you suffer from an injury to your elbow when something fell and landed directly on it. You get it checked out medically, and the doctor says that it primarily involves bruising and soft tissue injuries. Since the injury occurred, it's been nearly impossible for you to take a shower, dress, or get a good night's sleep. You also have a lot of pain with your elbow injury. After a month, the pain still hasn't gone down much. You still can't change your clothes, shower, or get a decent night's sleep.

For some reason, the pain continues the next month and then the next month. By now, you're at your wit's end about this pain. You're seeing how much it's affecting your life and your loved ones, making you angry, frustrated, resentful, and miserable.

And since these emotions never return to neutrality, you are constantly irritable. You find yourself snapping at family members even though you have never done this before. The chronic pain has become something you experience––it's a sensory experience––and has been messing with your emotions as well. Until this chronic pain is totally resolved, you have no hope that anything will get any better. You can't discharge the emotions about the situation.

What Happens Physiologically with Chronic Pain

Emotions and stress can worsen chronic pain in significant ways. When stressed or anxious, your body releases stress hormones like cortisol. While cortisone and other stress hormones are essential for handling acute stress, prolonged exposure can lead to increased sensitivity to pain.

Cortisol and stress can also cause other things to happen in the body. Cortisol and stress can cause muscle tension, which worsens existing pain. They can slow down digestion, increase blood pressure, increase breathing rate and heartbeat, and cause sweating. They can also raise blood sugar levels.

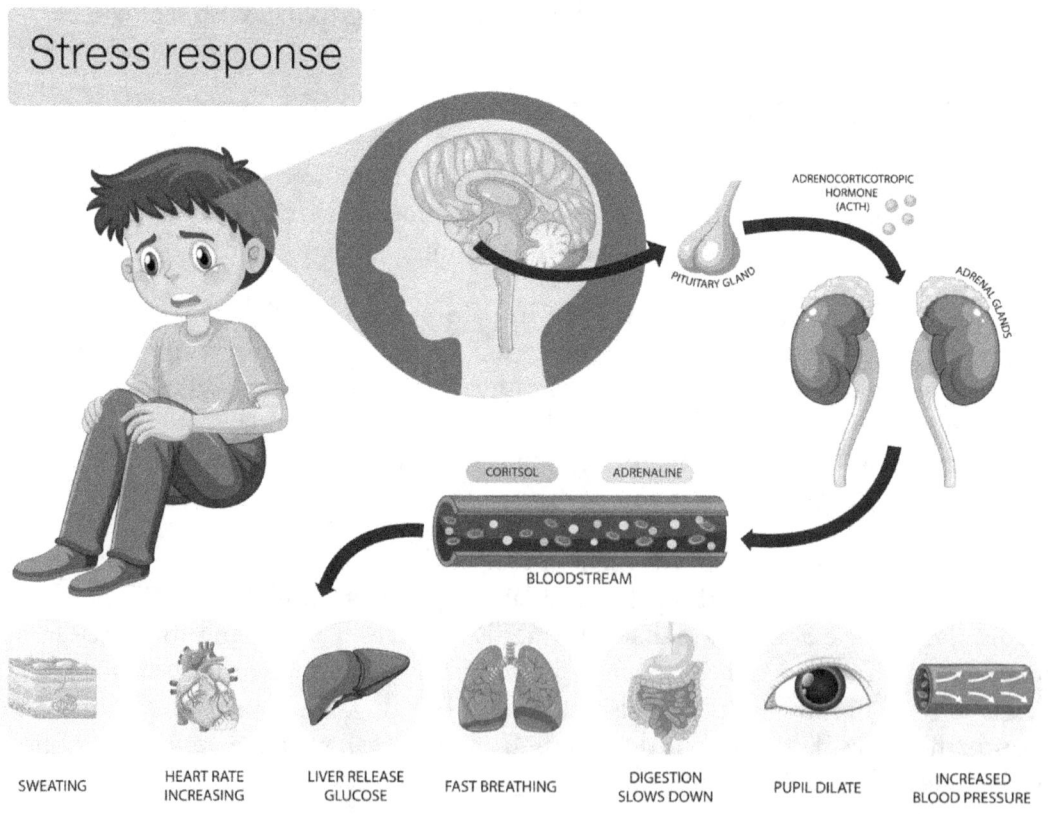

The stress response is a programmed body response that involves the pituitary gland, adrenal glands, bloodstream, skin, heart, liver, lungs, GI tract, eyes, and blood vessels. ACTH, cortisol, and adrenaline are created, which cause sweating, increase in heart rate, glucose increases, fast breathing, digestion slowing, dilation of the pupils, and increased blood pressure. If this stress response is felt often enough, these changes are occurring on a continual basis, which cause harm.

One thing that is unique about this interrelationship is that someone with chronic back pain might find that their pain worsens during periods of high stress, making it difficult to pinpoint a purely physical cause. All their trips to the doctor may not uncover the true cause of the back problem.

This interplay between the mind and body makes it clear that addressing chronic pain requires a holistic approach that considers both physical and emotional factors. By not addressing the pain, the situation becomes an unresolved trauma in the body. Unresolved trauma can end up manifesting as chronic pain in the body, creating a complex web of physical and emotional suffering. It can appear in various forms, such as fibromyalgia, tension headaches, or unexplained muscle pain.

Fibromyalgia is a condition characterized by widespread pain and tenderness, often linked to past emotional trauma. Tension headaches can be triggered by unresolved stress or anxiety, causing debilitating pain that affects daily life.

These things occur because your body's autonomic nervous system, which is responsible for the fight-or-flight response, can become stuck in a heightened state of alert. This constant state of readiness can lead to chronic muscle tension. Whenever your muscles are tense and won't relax, there will be persistent pain.

The cycle of pain and stress creates a feedback loop that perpetuates chronic pain. So it's all your body's fault for why this happens! You aren't creating this feedback loop. Your body is programmed with it. But it's up to you to re-train it.

Other things happen automatically in your body from the cycle of pain. Pain causes your body to produce stress hormones like cortisol more often and even continuously, which can increase your perception of pain. This heightened pain perception, in turn, leads to more stress, creating a vicious cycle.

Chronic stress can also cause your muscles to stay tense, leading to increased pain and discomfort. Your brain plays a significant role in this cycle, as it can become conditioned to expect pain, perpetuating the sensation even without an apparent cause. This pain-stress cycle can make it challenging to break free from chronic pain without addressing both the physical and emotional aspects. But it's not impossible, and many people have done it!

There is an Answer!

Breaking this cycle with Somatic Awareness offers a promising approach to managing chronic pain. Somatic Awareness involves becoming more attuned to your body and its sensations, allowing you to identify and address areas of tension and discomfort. Techniques for increasing body awareness include Body Scanning, Mindfulness practices, and Gentle Movement exercises discussed in earlier chapters. These practices help you tune into your body's signals, making it easier to identify and release areas of tension.

Mindfulness plays a crucial role in pain reduction by helping you stay in the present and focused on the moment rather than becoming overwhelmed by pain or stress. Mindfulness practices, such as Meditation and Deep Breathing, can help calm the nervous system, reducing pain perception and thus overall pain.

You've already learned how to do the body scanning technique. Below is how it can be adapted for pain awareness

How to Do Body Scanning for Pain Awareness

1. Find a quiet, comfortable space where you won't be disturbed.

2. Lie down or sit comfortably and close your eyes.

3. Start by focusing on your breath, taking slow, deep breaths to center yourself.

4. Begin the Body Scan at the top of your head, slowly moving your attention down through your body.

5. Notice any pain, tension, or discomfort areas without judgment.

6. Breathe into these areas, imagining your breath flowing into them and them relaxing.

7. Continue the scan down to your toes, taking time to experience each sensation fully.

8. Reflect on any insights or patterns you notice during the scan.

Using Somatic Awareness to break the pain-stress cycle can significantly improve pain management. By becoming more attuned to your body and addressing pain's physical and emotional components, you can find relief and improve your mental and physical health.

Somatic Exercises for Chronic Pain Relief

Somatic exercises help you become aware of your body and its sensations, which can be incredibly beneficial for managing chronic pain. Unlike traditional workouts, the purpose of these exercises isn't to build muscle or burn calories. Instead, they focus on releasing tension, improving body awareness, and encouraging relaxation. The benefits are extensive, from reducing muscle stiffness to alleviating pain and improving overall quality of life.

Simple Gentle Stretches

One of the most effective somatic exercises for pain relief is Simple Gentle Stretching. These routines are designed to be slow and mindful, allowing you to focus on your body's sensations.

Here's how to do them:

1. Start with simple neck stretches.

2. Sit comfortably and gently tilt your head to one side, bringing your ear towards your shoulder.

3. Hold for a few breaths.

4. Then switch sides.

5. Move on to shoulder rolls by lifting your shoulders towards your ears and then rolling them back and down. This can help release tension that often accumulates in the neck and shoulders.

6. For your lower body, try seated forward bends. Sit with your legs extended in front of you and slowly reach your toes, going only as far as comfortable. These gentle stretches can help alleviate muscle tightness and improve flexibility.

Progressive Muscle Relaxation

It's probably no surprise to you that Progressive Muscle Relaxation (PMR) can be tailored to chronic pain. As you may remember from earlier in this book, PMR involves tensing and relaxing different muscle groups to release tension and reduce pain.

Here's how to do the PMR Method for Chronic Pain:

1. Lie down on a yoga mat or a comfortable pad.

2. Start with the muscles in your toes. Tense your toes as tight as you can. Hold the tenseness for 3 to 5 seconds, feeling what it feels like to have this intense tightness in your toes.

3. Slowly release the tension.

4. Next, tense the muscles in your feet as tightly as possible for 3-5 seconds. Then, slowly release the tension.

5. Move up to your calves and repeat this process.

6. Then go to your thighs and so on until you've worked your way up to your head.

7. Pay special attention to areas where you experience chronic pain, spending extra time tensing and relaxing those muscles.

This practice not only helps in reducing muscle tension but also brings a sense of calm and relaxation.

How to Integrate These Exercises Into Your Day

Integrating Somatic Exercises into your daily life can significantly improve your pain levels. Here's an idea of what your day could look like:

Time	Exercise	Comment
Morning	Stretches to loosen up your body such as neck stretches and shoulder rolls	Stretches may be done anywhere.
Mid-day	Body scans for pain	Take a few minutes to do this. Address any area of discomfort and pain.
Evening	Relaxation Routine	Reducing pain before sleep is the goal.
Gentle Stretches	Progressive Muscle Relaxation	This method has stood the test of time.
Pain flare-ups during the day	Any exercise to bring relief immediately	You can also use multiple the day exercises for maximum effectiveness.

Adapting Exercises for Limited Mobility

Adapting these exercises to your individual needs is crucial for their effectiveness. If you have limited mobility, you can modify stretches to suit your capabilities.

Here are tips for you if you have limited mobility.

1. If you can't reach your toes during a forward bend, use a strap or towel to extend your reach.

2. Props like pillows and blankets can provide additional support, making exercises more comfortable.

3. Gradually increase the intensity and duration of your exercises as you become more comfortable.

4. Start with short sessions and slowly build up to longer ones.

5. Always listen to your body's signals and adjust your routine accordingly.

6. If an exercise causes pain, modify or skip it altogether. The goal is to create a good practice that supports your healing.

These Somatic Exercises have been beneficial for me. They have helped me manage my chronic pain, improve my general wellness, and allow me to move with more agility and less stiffness. Using them daily in your routine can bring similar benefits, allowing you to live a more comfortable and fulfilling life.

Neuroplasticity: Rewiring the Brain for Pain Management

Neuroplasticity was something discussed earlier in this book. It refers to the brain's ability to change and adapt throughout life. This incredible flexibility allows us to learn new skills, recover from injuries, and manage chronic pain.

Neuroplasticity means that your brain can form new neural connections and pathways in response to your experiences and behaviors. This adaptability is crucial when altering how we perceive and manage pain.

Now, here's a fact that really hit me hard: Chronic pain doesn't just affect your body; it changes your brain. Chronic pain can actually cause atrophy—or withering up—of the hippocampus. This has been found to cause problems such as difficulty concentrating and a bad memory. According to researchers at the University of Chinese Academy of Sciences in Beijing in 2023, it's also associated with dementia.

Yes, that means if you have chronic pain, especially in multiple areas of your body, you can expect that your brain is shrinking away.

But don't become distraught about the brain atrophy! Canadian scientists found that pain relief normalizes the withering away of the hippocampus. This is why you really MUST address your chronic pain––and using Somatic Therapy, you have a solution to do it.

Because of neuroplasticity, over time, the brain can become conditioned to expect pain, creating a self-perpetuating cycle. This is because of the structural and functional changes within the brain.

For example, areas responsible for processing pain signals can become more active, making you more sensitive to pain. Additionally, negative thought patterns can reinforce pain pathways, making it harder to break free from chronic pain. When you consistently experience pain, your brain strengthens its neural connections, making the pain feel even more real and persistent.

How to Rewire Your Brain

Several practical techniques can help you rewire the brain. Mindfulness Meditation, Cognitive Restructuring, and Visualization are three of the top ways to do this.

1. **Mindfulness Meditation** is a powerful tool for reducing pain perception. By focusing on the present moment and observing your thoughts and sensations without judgment, you can train your brain to respond differently to pain. Regular practice can help decrease the brain's reactivity to pain signals, making the experience of pain less intense.

2. **Cognitive Restructuring** involves changing negative thought patterns that reinforce pain. This could mean challenging thoughts like "I'll never get better" and replacing them with more positive, realistic ones. Over time, this can weaken the neural pathways associated with pain and build new, healthier ones.

3. **Visualization Techniques** are used to release tension, decrease pain, and increase the sense of relaxation. They are a powerful way to create positive neural pathways.

The Visualization I have used is one that centered on a peaceful place I often revisit in my mind. By focusing fully on this image, I could feel my body relax. The tension and the pain in my body began to melt away.

When I first started using visualization, I struggled with my mind constantly wandering from one thought to another. It took patience and consistent effort to redirect my focus back to the visualization. With time and regular practice, it gradually became easier. If you remain consistent, you're likely to see similar progress. Remember, patience and persistence are essential, especially if this is a new exercise for you.

By imagining yourself pain-free, you can train your brain to focus on positive sensations rather than pain.

For instance, picture yourself walking on a beach, feeling the warm sand under your feet and the gentle breeze on your face. This mental imagery can activate the same neural circuits as the actual experience, helping to shift your focus away from pain. Regular practice of these techniques can significantly change how your brain processes pain, making it easier to manage.

Proof About These Techniques

The science backing these techniques is compelling. Numerous studies have demonstrated the effectiveness of neuroplasticity-based approaches in managing chronic pain. For instance, research on Mindfulness Meditation has shown that it can reduce pain intensity and improve balanced well-being.

Below are links to some of the research that has been conducted on the validity of these techniques. They also offer contact information if you desire medical guidance in starting this therapy.

- https://www.healthpartners.com/blog/treat-pain-without-pills/

- https://southernpainclinic.com/blog/5-proven-relaxation-techniques-to-reduce-chronic-pain/

Other studies have been done regarding the effectiveness of Visualization techniques. In 2015, a systematic review of the effects of Guided Imagery for arthritis and other rheumatic diseases that was published in the *Pain Management in Nursing* medical journal. They analyzed seven studies with 306 total participants with an average age of 63 years old with different conditions such as fibromyalgia and arthritis and found the following:

- Significant reductions in pain and mobility difficulties at week 12

- Significant increases in quality of health at week 12 compared to the control group

- Significant reductions in anxiety

- Improved pain perception

- Ability to manage pain and other symptoms increased significantly.

In another study, doctors in Indonesia tested the effectiveness of Guided Imagery on pain intensity in breast cancer patients. They found a reduction in pain that was accompanied by decreased pulse rate and blood pressure. This means the body was attempting to return to parasympathetic nervous system functioning, where it could heal and regenerate.

When Guided Imagery was taught to children and adults, it was found to be effective in relieving the anxiety that children had before an operation as well as in adults. Guided Imagery also decreased the postoperative pain in the adults tested. This study was a meta-analysis study of 21 medical records that appeared in the medical journal called *Complementary Therapeutic Clinical Practices* in 2020.

An overview easy-to-read article on these studies may be found here: https://www.pathways.health/blog/visualization-guided-imagery-for-pain-relief/

When brain imaging was included in this type of study, doctors have found that the brain is making more robust neural connections in the brain areas associated with positive emotions and pain modulation. These findings align with the concept that your brain can be trained to focus on positive experiences, reducing the impact of chronic pain.

In my experience, integrating these neuroplasticity techniques has made a difference. I started with Mindfulness Meditation while working with a meditation coach, dedicating just a few minutes each day to focus on my breath and observe my thoughts. As part of that process, visualization was a key component of training my brain to shift from the negative track that seemed never to stop running to more positive and hope-filled images. Gradually, I noticed a shift in how I perceived pain and my life in general. Both became less overwhelming and more manageable.

Adding Cognitive Restructuring helped me challenge negative thoughts that often exacerbated my pain. Visualization exercises further reinforced positive neural pathways, making it easier to cope with daily discomfort. These practices have improved my overall outlook on life.

Titration: Gradual Exposure to Heal Chronic Pain

For Somatic Therapy, Titration breaking down overwhelming or distressing experiences into small, manageable pieces to avoid re-traumatization or overwhelm. This doesn't mean you dive headfirst into lots of discomfort but that you take small, manageable steps to face those triggers.

This allows you to process traumatic memories or sensations in a way that feels safe and tolerable, gradually allowing the nervous system to release stored energy or emotions without being flooded. The benefits of Titration for chronic pain management are significant. Slowly increasing your exposure to pain sensations can reduce their intensity over time. This helps desensitize the nervous system, making it less reactive to pain stimuli and more equipped to handle stress without added pain medications.

Main Differences

Aspect	Pendulation	Titration
Focus	Oscillating between states of activation and calm	Addressing trauma in small, manageable doses
Purpose	To build resilience and tolerance for discomfort	To prevent overwhelm and safely process trauma
Metaphor	Swinging like a pendulum between opposites	Adding small drops of dye to water
Nervous System	Teaches the system how to return to safety from stress	Prevents flooding or overstimulation

Mindful, Gradual Exposure to Pain Sensations

One effective technique for Titration involves Mindful, Gradual Exposure to Pain Sensations.

Here's the procedure:

1. Start by finding a quiet space where you can sit comfortably.

2. Close your eyes and take a few deep breaths to center yourself.

3. Focus on a specific area of your body where you feel pain. Rather than trying to avoid the sensation, gently bring your attention to it.

4. Notice the quality of the pain—its intensity, location, and other characteristics. Spend a few moments with this sensation.

5. Then shift your focus to a part of your body that feels neutral or pleasant (one where there's no pain).

6. Repeat the process until the pain diminishes.

This back-and-forth movement helps your nervous system learn to regulate itself, reducing the overall perception of pain.

Mix Pendulation with Titration or Breathing

Using Pendulation with Titration is another powerful method. Pendulation involves moving between discomfort and comfort, helping build resilience. Here's how they work together:

Pendulation can be used during titration to ensure the client doesn't get stuck in activation. For instance, while processing a small piece of trauma, the therapist might help the client shift to a calmer state before addressing the next piece. Together, these techniques allow the nervous system to process trauma safely, integrating challenging sensations or memories in a way that builds capacity and promotes healing.

Here's how to do it:

1. Focus on a painful sensation for a short period.

2. Shift your attention to a part of your body that feels good or neutral.

3. If your pain returns prominent in your mind, repeat the process by shifting your attention again. You may need to do this several times.

4. These exercises will require patience. The pain may be persistent and you may need many sessions of these exercises until it has diminished enough to be manageable.

This oscillation helps your body and mind learn that it's possible to experience pain without being overwhelmed.

Combining this with Breathwork can further enhance the calming effects. As you focus on a painful area, take slow, deep breaths. Imagine each breath bringing relief and relaxation to the painful location. This can help soothe your body and mind, making the sensation more manageable.

Titration techniques can be applied in various aspects of daily life. For instance, if certain stressful situations exacerbate your pain, you can use Titration to increase your exposure to these situations gradually. Start by facing the problem briefly, then take a break to do something calming. Gradually increase the length of time you spend in a stressful situation, always balancing it with periods of relaxation. This approach can help desensitize your nervous system to the stressor, reducing its impact on your pain levels.

Similarly, you can use Titration during physical activities that cause pain. If walking for extended periods triggers your pain, start with short walks and gradually extend the duration as your body adapts.

Decrease Emotional Triggers with Titration

Emotional triggers related to pain can also be managed using Titration techniques. If specific memories or thoughts intensify your pain, start by briefly bringing them to mind in a safe, controlled environment. Pair this exposure with Grounding Exercises or Breathwork to help manage the emotional response. Over time, you can increase the length and intensity of the exposure, allowing your nervous system to adapt without becoming overwhelmed.

Combine Titration with Body Awareness Exercises

Integrating Titration with other somatic practices can enhance its effectiveness. For example, you can combine Titration with Body Awareness Exercises to increase your overall sensitivity to bodily sensations. As you practice gradual exposure, pay attention to how your body responds and adjust your approach accordingly.

Combine Titration with Grounding Techniques

Combining Titration with Grounding techniques can provide additional stability. Before and after exposing yourself to pain triggers, take a moment to ground yourself by noticing the sensation of your feet on the ground or holding an object with a reassuring texture. This can help anchor you and provide a sense of safety.

Titration Adds Benefits to Your Pain Management Plan

Adding Titration can significantly benefit a holistic pain management routine. Use it alongside other somatic practices like Body Scanning, Progressive Muscle Relaxation, and Mindfulness Meditation. You can achieve more effective and lasting relief by creating a balanced approach that addresses pain's physical and emotional aspects.

Summary

Titration offers a gentle yet powerful way to build resilience and reduce pain intensity over time. By gradually exposing yourself to pain triggers in a controlled manner, you can help your nervous system adapt and become less reactive. This approach and other somatic practices can provide a comprehensive strategy for managing chronic pain and improving wellness.

Here are the summary charts for the somatic exercises in this chapter.

Exercise	Ease of Practice	Time Commitment
Body Scanning for Pain Awareness	Moderate	5–10 mins
Mindfulness Meditation	Easy	10 mins
Cognitive Restructuring	Moderate	5 mins
Visualization Techniques	Easy	5–10 mins
Gentle Stretches	Easy	5–10 mins
Progressive Muscle Relaxation	Moderate	20–25 mins
Titration Techniques	Moderate	5–10 mins
Pendulation Techniques	Moderate	5–10 mins
Mindful Gradual Exposure	Moderate	5 mins
Combining Titration with Grounding and Breathwork	Moderate	10 mins

Exercise	Relaxation	Manage Stress	Instant Calm	Regulates Emotions	Better Sleep	Clear Mind
Body Scanning for Pain Awareness	✓	✓	✓	✓	✓	✓
Mindfulness Meditation	✓	✓	✓	✓	✓	✓
Cognitive Restructuring	✓	✓		✓		✓
Visualization Techniques	✓	✓	✓	✓		✓

Exercise	Relaxation	Manage Stress	Instant Calm	Regulates Emotions	Better Sleep	Clear Mind
Gentle Stretches	✓	✓	✓	✓	✓	✓
Progressive Muscle Relaxation	✓	✓	✓	✓		✓
Titration Techniques	✓	✓		✓		✓
Pendulation Techniques	✓	✓	✓	✓		✓

Exercise	Relaxation	Manage Stress	Instant Calm	Regulates Emotions	Better Sleep	Clear Mind
Mindful Gradual Exposure	✓	✓	✓	✓		✓
Combining Titration with Grounding and Breathwork	✓	✓	✓	✓		✓

In a later chapter, we will explore integrating these practices into a supportive community, fostering connections, and building a network of encouragement and understanding. First, let's read some true-life success stories that somatic participants have enjoyed.

Make a Difference with Your Review

Unlock the Power of Generosity

"The best way to find yourself is to lose yourself in the service of others." – Mahatma Gandhi

Helping others brings a sense of joy that's hard to match. Would you join me in spreading that joy?

Imagine someone, just like you, looking for simple, practical ways to manage stress, rebuild resilience, and feel more at peace. Your review could be the guiding light they need to begin their journey.

My goal with *Body Wisdom through Somatic Therapy* is to make the tools for healing and connection easy and accessible for everyone. But to reach more people, I need your help.

When someone chooses a book, they often rely on reviews. A few kind words from you could:

- Help someone take their first step toward healing.

- Encourage another person to rebuild their resilience.

- Inspire someone to reconnect with their body and inner peace.

- Bring more light into someone's life.

It costs nothing, takes just a moment, but could change everything for someone searching for hope.

Simply scan the QR code or visit the link below to share your thoughts.

https://www.amazon.com/review/review-your-purchases/?asin=B0DSLWC8KG

If this book has helped you in any way, I'd love to hear about it—and so would others.

Thank you for being a part of this journey. Your generosity means the world to me.

Warmly,
Grace Bailey

Chapter 6

PERSONAL STORIES AND CASE STUDIES

Healing is a journey, not a destination.

-- DEVIN JUSTESEN

PERSONAL STORIES MEAN A lot to just about everything---personal relationships, business relationships, family, and learning anything new. I want to share the stories of Jane, Mark, Tom, and Sarah and how they used Somatic Therapy to change their lives.

Jane's journey is a testament to the resilience of the human spirit. It also shows the profound impact that reconnecting with your body can have on your positive wellness success story.

Jane grew up in a small town in a household filled with tension and fear. From a young age, she experienced emotional trauma and physical abuse. These early experiences left deep scars, both mentally and physically. As a result, Jane struggled with anxiety, depression, and chronic pain for most of her adult life.

She tried various forms of traditional therapy, hoping to find relief. While talk therapy helped her understand her experiences, it didn't fully address the physical manifestations of her trauma. She often felt like something was missing, a piece of the puzzle that could bring her the peace she desperately sought.

During a particularly challenging period, Jane's therapist suggested she try Somatic Therapy. At first, Jane was hesitant and skeptical. How could focusing on her body help with the emotional turmoil she felt inside?

Despite her doubts, she decided to give it a try. Her first session was a revelation. The therapist guided her through a Body Scan, a simple exercise that involved paying attention to different parts of her body and noticing any sensations. For the first time in years, Jane felt a connection to her body that she hadn't realized was missing. She noticed areas of tension she had been carrying for years and began to understand how her body held onto the trauma she had experienced.

Mental Health Changes Occurred Quickly

As Jane continued with Somatic Therapy, she was introduced to various techniques that helped her manage her anxiety and regulate her emotions. Grounding Exercises became a vital part of her routine. These exercises enabled her to stay present and connected to the moment. This reduced the overwhelming feelings of anxiety that often plagued her.

She found a sense of stability and calm by focusing on the sensation of her feet on the ground or the texture of an object in her hand. Breathwork also played a significant role in her healing. Learning to control her breath allowed her to regulate emotional responses and find relief from intense waves of anxiety that would sometimes wash over her. Techniques like Diaphragmatic Breathing and the 4-7-8 Method became tools she relied on during moments of distress.

Reducing Muscle Tension

Another critical technique in Jane's healing journey was Progressive Muscle Relaxation. She tensed and relaxed different muscle groups, which released the tension that had built up in her body over the years. By systematically working through each muscle group, she learned to identify areas of chronic tension and release them, which in turn alleviated some of her physical pain. These techniques helped Jane develop a deeper awareness of her body and its responses to stress and trauma. She began to understand the intricate connection between her mind and body and how addressing one could positively impact the other.

Lessened PTSD, Stress Handled

The outcomes of Jane's Somatic Therapy journey were nothing short of transformative. Her PTSD symptoms, which had once been debilitating, began to lessen. She found she was more emotionally stable and better able to handle the stresses of daily life. The chronic pain that had plagued her for years started to subside, and she felt a newfound sense of safety and self-awareness.

Jane often reflected on her journey with a sense of awe and gratitude. She realized the missing piece she had been searching for was a deeper connection to her body. By learning to listen to her body's signals and respond with compassion and care, she found a path to healing that resonated with her profoundly.

Reflection Exercise: Jane's Journey

1. Reflect on a time when you felt disconnected from your body. What were the circumstances, and how did it impact your mental and physical health?

2. Consider any techniques you've tried previously to manage stress or anxiety. What worked, and what didn't?

3. Think about the concept of Somatic Therapy. How do you feel about the idea of using body awareness to address emotional and physical pain?

4. Write down any area of your body where you often feel tension or discomfort. Reflect on what emotions might be associated with these sensations.

Jane's story is a powerful reminder that healing is possible, even after years of suffering.

Her journey highlights the importance of reconnecting with our bodies and listening to their wisdom. Through Somatic Therapy, Jane found a path to healing that addressed both her emotional and physical pain, transforming her life in ways she never thought possible.

Rebuilding Resilience: Mark's Path to Healing

Mark was the kind of person who seemed to have it all together. With a high-powered job in a fast-paced corporate environment, he thrived on deadlines and challenges. Yet, beneath his calm exterior, he was struggling. The constant stress and pressure were taking a toll on him. He began to experience burnout and chronic stress symptoms, such as insomnia, irritability, and frequent headaches. Mark tried to cope in various ways, including using substances like alcohol to unwind after long days. But these coping mechanisms only provided temporary relief and often left him feeling worse. He knew he needed a more sustainable solution.

A colleague first suggested Somatic Therapy to Mark. Intrigued but skeptical, he decided to investigate it. He had tried traditional therapy before but found it didn't fully address the physical symptoms of his stress.

His first session with a Somatic Therapist was eye-opening. He walked in with a mix of resistance and curiosity, unsure what to expect. The therapist led him through a series of Gentle Exercises designed to help him become more aware of his body. Mark was surprised that even Simple Movements and Breathing techniques brought relief he hadn't experienced in years. For the first time, he felt a glimmer of hope that things could change.

Mark's initial breakthroughs came through the practice of Pendulation exercises. These exercises helped him manage his stress by teaching him to move between states of calm and discomfort. The therapist explained that this technique could help his nervous system learn to regulate itself more effectively.

Mark started with small, manageable steps, focusing on areas of his body that felt safe and relaxed before gradually moving his attention to areas of tension. This back–and–forth movement became a powerful tool, allowing him to face his stress without becoming overwhelmed. It was like discovering a new way to navigate through the chaos of his mind and body.

Another technique that proved invaluable for Mark was Mindful Movement. Unlike traditional exercise routines, Mindful Movement focused on slow, deliberate actions, encouraging him to tune into his body's sensations. He would spend a few minutes each morning doing Gentle Stretches and paying close attention to how his muscles felt. This practice helped him start his day with a sense of calm and presence, setting a positive tone for the hours ahead.

Visualization Techniques also played a significant role in his healing process. Mark learned to create a safe space in his mind where he felt completely at ease. Whenever he felt overwhelmed, he would close his eyes and imagine himself in this tranquil setting, allowing his body and mind to relax.

The results of Mark's Somatic Therapy were profound. Over time, he noticed a significant increase in his resilience and ability to tolerate stress. The burnout symptoms that had once plagued him began to diminish, and he found himself with more energy and a clearer mind. His work-life balance improved, allowing him to enjoy his job without feeling constantly overwhelmed. Mark's reflections on his progress were filled with gratitude. He realized that Somatic Therapy had given him tools to not only manage his stress but also to build a deeper connection with himself. Instead, he no longer relied on unhealthy coping mechanisms and embraced practices that nurtured his well-being.

Mark often spoke about the sense of empowerment he felt through Somatic Therapy. He had learned to listen to his body and respond with compassion and care. This newfound awareness transformed his approach to both work and personal life. He became more present and engaged with his tasks and those around him. The techniques he learned in Somatic Therapy became integral to his daily routine, helping him maintain balance and peace. Mark's story is a testament to the power of resilience-building techniques and their profound impact on one's life.

Chronic Pain Management: Sarah's Success Story

Sarah was grappling with the daily torment of fibromyalgia, a chronic condition characterized by widespread pain and fatigue. Her life had been turned upside down by this diagnosis. Every morning, she woke up feeling like she hadn't slept, her body aching from head to toe. Simple tasks became monumental challenges. She tried various forms of pain management, including medication and physical therapy, but found little relief. Each day felt like a battle, and she was growing increasingly desperate for a solution that could offer even a glimmer of hope.

Sarah's exploration of Somatic Therapy began at the suggestion of a support group she attended for chronic pain sufferers. Initially, she was skeptical. The idea that focusing on her body's sensations could alleviate pain seemed far-fetched.

Her first few sessions didn't bring the immediate results she had hoped for, which only fueled her doubts. However, something kept her going back. Perhaps it was the sense of community she felt with others who understood her plight, or maybe it was the gentle encouragement from her therapist. Despite her reservations, Sarah persevered through those early sessions, slowly beginning to see the potential for change.

One of the first techniques Sarah embraced was a series of Gentle Stretching routines. Unlike the rigorous exercises she had tried in physical therapy, these movements were slow and mindful, designed to increase her body awareness and release tension. She learned to focus on the sensations in her muscles, noticing how they responded to each stretch. This practice helped her reconnect with her body in a way she hadn't experienced before.

Progressive Muscle Relaxation became another cornerstone of her routine. By systematically tensing and relaxing different muscle groups, Sarah found she could reduce the chronic tension that had plagued her for years. This technique not only alleviated her pain but also helped her identify specific areas where she held stress.

Breathwork was another powerful tool in Sarah's arsenal. She learned to use deep, Diaphragmatic Breathing to manage pain flare-ups. During these episodes, she would focus on taking slow, deep breaths, allowing her body to relax and release the tension that often accompanies her pain. Visualization Techniques also played a significant role in her pain management strategy. Sarah would close her eyes and imagine a warm, soothing light enveloping her body, melting away the pain. This mental imagery provided her with a sense of comfort and control, offering a respite from her constant discomfort.

The impact of Somatic Therapy on Sarah's life was life changing. Over time, she experienced a significant reduction in her pain levels. She no longer felt like a prisoner in her own body. Her daily functioning improved dramatically, allowing her to engage in activities she had once thought impossible. Walking her dog or cooking a meal became a source of joy rather than stress.

Sarah often reflected on her Somatic Therapy journey with gratitude. She realized that while the process had been slow and, at times, frustrating, it had also been incredibly rewarding. She had learned to listen to her body and respond with compassion, a skill that had far-reaching benefits beyond pain management.

Sarah's success story is a powerful reminder of the healing potential within us all. Her perseverance and openness to new approaches allowed her to find relief in a way she had never imagined. Through Somatic Therapy, Sarah not only managed her chronic pain but also reclaimed her life, finding a sense of peace and well-being that had long eluded her. Her journey underscores the importance of patience, determination, and a willingness to explore new paths to healing.

Emotional Regulation: Tom's Transformation

Tom's story is one of navigating the choppy waters of intense emotions and mood swings. From a young age, he experienced fluctuations in his emotional state that were challenging to manage. These mood swings affected his personal relationships, leading to misunderstandings and conflicts. His intense emotions often resulted in unproductive days and strained interactions with his work colleagues.

Tom tried various methods to control his emotions, including traditional therapy and medication, but found little lasting relief. His life felt like a rollercoaster ride that never ended. Each day brought new challenges that left him feeling exhausted and defeated.

Tom was introduced to Somatic Therapy through a referral from his psychologist, who noticed that traditional methods weren't providing the relief Tom needed. Initially, like many new to Somatic Therapy, Tom was resistant. Focusing on physical sensations to manage his emotions seemed foreign and, frankly, odd. His first few sessions were met with skepticism. He found it difficult to let go of his analytical mind and trust the process.

However, his therapist was patient, guiding him through the exercises and encouraging him to stay open. Small breakthroughs began to happen. During one session, Tom experienced a moment of clarity while practicing a simple breathwork exercise. For the first time in a long while, he felt a sense of calm wash over him, giving him a glimpse of what was possible.

Breathwork became a cornerstone of Tom's emotional regulation toolkit. He learned techniques like Diaphragmatic Breathing and the 4-7-8 Method, which provided immediate relief during moments of intense emotion. Focusing on his breath could calm his nervous system, reducing the intensity of his emotional responses.

Body Awareness practices also played a crucial role. Tom was guided to tune into his body's sensations, noticing areas of tension and discomfort. This awareness helped him identify the physical manifestations of his emotions, allowing him to address them more effectively. Grounding Exercises were another critical component. Whenever Tom felt overwhelmed, he would focus on the sensation of his feet on the ground or the texture of an object in his hand. These exercises helped him stay present and centered, reducing the risk of being swept away by his emotions.

Emotional Labeling and Journaling were also integral to Tom's progress. By naming his emotions, he created a sense of distance, making them more manageable. He would write about his feelings and their physical sensations, gaining insights into his emotional patterns. This practice helped him understand his emotions better and provided a healthy outlet for expressing them.

The transformation Tom experienced was remarkable. Over time, he noticed significant improvements in his emotional stability and regulation. The mood swings that once dominated his life became less frequent and less intense. His relationships improved as he learned to respond to conflicts calmly and with understanding. His newfound emotional stability at work allowed him to be more productive and present.

Tom often reflected on the positive impact of his Somatic Therapy journey. He realized that the techniques he learned helped him manage his emotions and enhanced his mental and physical well-being. He felt more self-aware and mindful, capable of navigating life's challenges with greater ease and resilience.

Tom often spoke about the profound impact Somatic Therapy had on his life. He appreciated the practical, actionable techniques that provided immediate relief and long-term benefits. The breathwork, Body Awareness Practices, Grounding Exercises, and Emotional Labeling gave him tools he could rely on in any situation. These practices became a natural part of his daily routine, helping him maintain balance and peace.

Tom's story is a powerful example of how Somatic Therapy can transform emotional struggles into opportunities for growth and healing. His journey underscores the importance of exploring new approaches and staying open to possibilities, even when they seem unfamiliar. Tom found a path to emotional regulation that resonated deeply with him, offering a way to navigate life with greater clarity and calm.

Chapter 7

TOOLS FOR SELF-HEALING

Your body hears everything your mind says.

-- NAOMI JUDD

REALIZING HOW MUCH OUR bodies hold onto daily stress is an integral part of the journey toward healing. The following tools can help us progress and change how stress affects us.

Mapping and Charting Your Body's Wisdom

Somatic Mapping is a transformative tool in Somatic Therapy that helps you understand the language of your body. At its core, Somatic Mapping involves creating a visual representation of your bodily sensations. Think of it as charting the physical manifestations of your emotions and experiences.

The goal of this practice is to increase your awareness of how stress, trauma, and emotions are stored in your body. By identifying and mapping your sensations, you will gain insights into your physical and emotional state, making it easier to address and release built-up tension.

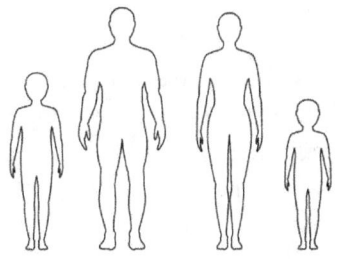

Outlines like these may be used for both front and back of the body as long as you label them "Front" or "Back." Choose the appropriate gender and age: young child, older child, or adult. Crop out the one you need and duplicate it.

<u>To begin Somatic Mapping, follow this procedure.</u>

1. First, find a body outline that you print online or that you draw yourself.

A body outline of the front of the body and an outline of the back of the body is what you are looking for. It can be a simple drawing or one that includes details such as where the breasts, pubic area, and collarbone are. The more detailed outlines make it easier to focus on specific areas of your body.

The outlines for the front of the bodies in this picture show sample outlines for two children of different ages: a man and a woman. More complex outlines are much more detailed.

If your health condition involves very specific parts of the body, you may want to use a drawing with labels as a guide for you when you do Body Scan techniques. These may or may not have internal organs listed.

Some outlines include a side view, which can be especially helpful if you are having side pain or issues that only occur on one side of the body.

Make sure the outline you choose matches your gender and your age. For example, you wouldn't choose a child's body outline if you were an adult, and you wouldn't choose a man's body outline if you were a woman. The diagrams serve as the canvas for your Somatic Map.

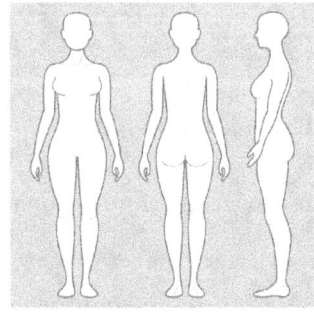

This outline representation for females also includes a side view, which may be helpful if you have pain on your side. Mark right or left on the side view.

2. With your body outline in front of you, find a quiet and comfortable space, such as a desk or a recliner, where you won't be disturbed.

3. Sit comfortably and take a few deep breaths to center yourself.

4. Focus on feeling your different body parts from head to toe. Which areas do you feel tension, pain, or other sensations? For instance, maybe there's a tightness in your chest or a heaviness in your legs. Mark these sensations on your diagram, using different colors or symbols to represent various feelings. Stripes may represent tightness, and heaviness may be represented by a solid color on the body part on the diagram.

This reflection can provide valuable insights into the connections between your physical sensations and emotional experiences. It's a process of self-discovery that can help you understand how your body responds to different stressors and emotions.

Practical applications of Somatic Mapping can be incredibly beneficial in daily life. For example, during moments of stress, take a few minutes to map your sensations. This can help you identify where your body is holding tension and give you a clearer picture of your stress response.

Over time, you can use these maps to track your progress and notice patterns in your bodily sensations. Bringing Somatic Maps to therapy sessions can also enhance your healing journey. Sharing your maps with your therapist can provide a visual tool to discuss your physical and emotional state, making it easier to address underlying issues.

Combine Somatic Mapping with Other Tools

Combining Somatic Mapping with other self-healing tools can amplify its benefits. For example, use Somatic Mapping alongside Journaling prompts to explore the connections between your physical sensations and emotions. Write about what you notice on your map and reflect on how these sensations relate to your daily experiences. This combination can deepen your self-awareness and provide a more comprehensive understanding of your body-mind connection.

Here's an example of this. On your Somatic Map, you color in a band of tightness on your back that corresponds to your bra line. You feel some tightness in your chest around your heart as well and color that area in. In your journal, you note that this happens when you eat a certain food or meal. The meal and food that instigates it is a comfort food. So, you think back to why you were eating that comfort food in the first place: it was because you were experiencing anxiety due to watching the news. The news report discussed the coming bad times. And you bought into the story, allowing it to affect your physiology.

In your journal, you also note that this tightness is immediately relieved when you get a chiropractic adjustment that addresses it.

Integrating Somatic Mapping with Body Awareness Exercises can enhance your practice. Before starting a Body Scan or Progressive Muscle Relaxation, take a few minutes to map your current sensations. This can help you focus on specific areas during your exercises, making them more effective.

Mindfulness practices also complement Somatic Mapping.

Here's how to integrate them below:

1. Before meditation, take out your Somatic Map and fill it out, highlighting the areas of concern.

2. Then prepare for meditation. Get in the proper position and make sure you are comfortable.

3. Review your Somatic Map, noting the areas of concern.

4. Notice how these areas feel.

5. Then breathe in deep breaths and relax.

6. Observe any changes in sensation in these areas as you breathe and relax.

This mindful approach can help you stay present and deepen your connection with your body. Somatic Mapping is a versatile and powerful tool that can enhance your self-healing journey. It provides a tangible way to understand and address the physical manifestations of your emotions, helping you cultivate greater awareness and well-being.

Resourcing Finds Strength in Positive Experiences

Resourcing involves identifying and utilizing positive experiences and internal strengths to build psychological resilience. Think of it as creating a toolkit filled with things that make you feel strong, safe, and supported. These resources can help stabilize you during times of stress or emotional upheaval. Knowing you can rely on this toolkit will boost your confidence in handling unforeseen stressors that arise in everyday life.

The role of positive experiences in this practice is crucial. They serve as anchors, helping you stay grounded and providing stability. By focusing on these positive aspects, you can cultivate emotional stability and strength, making it easier to navigate challenging situations.

How to do Resourcing:

1. Reflect on past positive experiences. Think about moments when you felt happy, calm, or proud. These can be significant events like a graduation or small moments like a peaceful walk in the park.

2. Identify supportive relationships in your life. These are the people who make you feel understood and valued.

3. Recognize your strengths and achievements, no matter how small they may seem. For example, you may be the type of person who stays calm under pressure, or you may have a knack for problem-solving.

4. Identify the activities that you find comfort in. These might be time spent in nature, artistic endeavors, crocheting, or other hobbies. Many people list activities like gardening, painting, or listening to music that provide immense emotional support for them.

5. Once you've identified your resources, it's time to learn how to use them effectively. Let's use Visualization. Close your eyes and vividly imagine a positive experience or a place where you feel safe and happy. This visualization can help you tap into the feelings of comfort and security associated with that memory.

Creating a resource list or collage can also be helpful. Write down or create visual representations of your identified resources and keep them somewhere accessible. Sensory reminders, such as a soothing scent or a comforting touch, can also be effective. For example, carrying a piece of fabric with a comforting texture or using a favorite essential oil can provide immediate relief. Engaging in activities that bring you joy and comfort, like reading a favorite book or taking a warm bath, can also serve as effective resources.

Using resourcing in your daily life is easy. Here's an example of how to incorporate them into your busy day.

Time of Day	Activity
Before dinner	Get out your Journal. Think of something good that happened. Write it down.
Stressful moments	Visualize one positive experience that you have written in your Journal.
	Continue thinking about this positive experience until you notice a shift in your thinking and feelings.
Troubled family member	Share some of your positive experiences with your loved one as a way to give encouragement.

For example, if you're feeling overwhelmed at work, take a moment to visualize a positive experience or use a sensory reminder. Sharing your resources with loved ones can also be incredibly beneficial. Discuss your positive experiences and strengths with friends or family and encourage them to do the same. This mutual support can strengthen your relationships and provide additional emotional stability.

Creating a Personal Healing Routine

A personal healing routine is a personalized, intentional approach to managing your well-being. It's a plan of what you are going to do. When you create a personal healing routine, you are making a commitment to treating yourself with kindness and compassion and keep your healing a priority. This type of plan is not fixed in stone but rather, it is flexible and evolves over time as your healing progresses.

The main components of a personal healing routine include the resources you have identified that you need to thrive physically, mentally, emotionally, and spiritually. It is your personal action steps to meet those needs. Take some time to visit this link to create and establish your routine. https://www.calm.com/blog/self-care-plan

If you ever watch YouTube videos or news reports of people who have healed themselves of horrible health problems, you may have noticed that they attribute their success to one or two major things, such as changing their diet or taking medication. What they never emphasize is probably the real reason why they got better—and that is consistency. Developing a routine of what is going to be done daily and sticking to it is one of those things they don't emphasize, but yet it's usually the big key to their success. If they didn't do these new things daily, they would not have success.

Consistency is vital when it comes to healing. By establishing a routine, you create a framework that supports your emotional and physical health. You take the time to work what you value into your daily schedule with a Personal Healing Routine.

This structured approach helps you build new, positive habits that can replace old, unhelpful ones. Over time, these habits become second nature, making it easier to maintain your well-being even during stressful times. Think of your healing routine as a personalized roadmap, guiding you toward a balanced and fulfilling life.

What's Included in a Personal Healing Routine?

A well-rounded Healing Routine includes several essential components, such as Body Awareness exercises, Breathwork, Grounding, Journaling, Visualization, Exercise, and other things you find important for your healing.

Daily Body Awareness Exercises are a great place to start. These exercises help you tune into your body and notice any areas of tension or discomfort.

Regular Breathwork and Grounding practices can further enhance this awareness, helping you stay present and calm.

Schedule time for self-reflection and Journaling. Writing down your thoughts and feelings can provide valuable insights and promote emotional processing.

Movement and Exercise are also crucial. Regular physical activity, such as yoga, walking, or dancing, can help release tension and improve overall mood.

Finally, set aside time for Resourcing and Relaxation. These moments of rest and self-care are vital for recharging your emotional and physical batteries.

Creating a custom healing routine that fits your individual needs and lifestyle is essential for its success. Start by assessing your personal needs and goals. What areas of your life need the most attention? What are your short-term and long-term goals? Once you clearly understand your needs, allocate specific times for each practice.

Here are some examples of Personal Healing Routines:

Time of Day	Routine 1 Exercises	Routine 2 Exercises
Mornings	Body Awareness Exercise	Breathing Exercises Stretching Body Scan
Evenings	Journaling Relaxation	Body Scan Visualization

Your routine will be adjusted frequently based on your progress. Whenever something in your life changes drastically, it will be time to tweak your Personal Healing Routine. Our lives are dynamic and change all the time. Finding a balance between self-care and other responsibilities no matter what is happening is what makes you a master at these techniques. Your routine should always support your well-being without adding extra stress.

How Do I Stay On Track?

Maintaining consistency in your healing routine can be a challenge at times, but there are practical strategies to help you stay on track. Here are my favorite tips and recommendations:

1. Always connect to the level of importance health has in your life. Considering how well you feel when you are doing XYZ is a good way to start. If you are having difficulty finding that importance, you might make a list of all the times you didn't give it a high priority and the results of that. This isn't to be misconstrued as a self-accusation exercise; instead, it is to provide a list of real-life circumstances that have brought you to where you are now. We all have made mistakes and acknowledging them is part of the healing process. Once you are convinced of the importance of taking health steps daily, you won't have to battle against will power to develop a healing routine.

2. Set reminders for yourself. Use planners to keep yourself organized and accountable.

3. Create a supportive environment by setting up a dedicated space for your practices. Sometimes people make a commitment in their mind to do things but then do not have what it takes to carry out that goal. For example, if you live in a tiny home, how can you expect stretching exercises to be comfortably done? The dedicated space needed for your practices could be a corner of your room with calming decorations and the necessary tools, such as a mat that conveniently fits on the floor in front of your bed or living room couch.

4. Seek accountability from friends or support groups. This can also be motivating. Sharing your goals with someone you trust and checking in with each other regularly is what makes this work.

5. Celebrate small successes and milestones to give yourself a sense of accomplishment and encouragement to keep going. Recognize your efforts and reward yourself for your dedication to your well-being.

Combining these strategies into your daily life can create a Healing Routine that supports your emotional and physical health.

Remember, the goal is to make self-care a regular and enjoyable part of your day. With consistency and dedication, your routines will help you navigate life's challenges with resilience and grace.

Journaling Prompts for Emotional Processing

Putting pen to paper offers a safe space to process feelings and gain clarity. Journaling provides numerous benefits for mental health. It helps you articulate your thoughts, making them more manageable.

When you're feeling overwhelmed, writing can release negative emotions, reducing stress and anxiety. Journaling aids in processing emotions by giving you a tangible way to explore and understand them. Writing out how you feel gives you the time and space to walk through the depth of your emotions. This allows you to see different aspects of the situation and reveals new insights as well. Journaling also fosters self-awareness and growth, allowing you to reflect on and learn from your experiences.

To make Journaling effective:

1. Start by finding a quiet and comfortable space to focus without distractions.

2. Set aside dedicated time for journaling, whether in the morning to set the tone for your day or in the evening to reflect. This could be anywhere from 30 minutes to 1 hour in most cases.

3. Write without self-censorship.

4. Let your thoughts flow freely without worrying about grammar or spelling.

This is your private space, and there are no rules. Using specific prompts can guide your reflections and make the practice more meaningful. You can find prompts online; just Google "prompts for ____". Prompts can help you delve deeper into your emotions and uncover insights you might not have reached otherwise.

Here are some specific journaling prompts to get you started. Reflecting on positive experiences and resources can be incredibly uplifting.

- Write about a recent positive experience, describing it in detail and reflecting on how it made you feel. Exploring physical sensations and their emotional meanings can deepen your body awareness. This is exceptionally helpful because it will add to your list of positive experiences that are used for other times.

- Describe a physical sensation you often experience, like tight shoulders, and explore what emotions might be connected to it.

- Writing about challenging emotions and how they manifest in the body can be cathartic. When you feel angry or sad, jot down where you feel it in your body and what might have triggered it. To determine what may have contributed to it, ask yourself what happened before ABC? What did I do in the two hours before ABC happened?

- Journaling about personal strengths and achievements can boost your confidence and self-esteem. List your strengths and recent achievements, no matter how small, and reflect on how they contribute to your well-being.

Daily Journaling in your daily routine can start small, dedicating just five to ten minutes a day. Make it a habit by integrating it into your routine, like your morning coffee or bedtime wind-down.

Keep your Journal in a location where you'll see it daily, reminding you to write. Use journaling as a tool during stressful moments. When you feel overwhelmed, jot down your thoughts and emotions briefly. You can always come back to them later and fill in more details. Over time, you'll find that regular Journaling can bring clarity and emotional stability, helping you navigate life's ups and downs more easily.

Another aspect of Journaling that many people use is to write about what happens specifically during their time of prayer. This is often a time when God speaks directly to someone, perhaps with instruction or correction. It is incredibly insightful for one's life and takes the process of Journaling to a whole new level.

The Emotion Code by Dr. Bradley Nelson

Dr. Bradley Nelson's book, *The Emotion Code,* is an excellent book that could make a big difference in restoring the mind-body connection.

This book offers a compelling approach to freeing your body from trapped emotions. As you already know, trapped emotions can profoundly affect your physical and emotional health. He introduces the concept of trapped emotions, describing them as emotional energies that get stuck in the body. While stuck, they influence your thoughts, feelings, and even physical well-being.

Emotions can become trapped from experiences you couldn't fully process when they happened. These could be traumatic events or times when you felt overwhelmed. These trapped emotions are similar to visceral fat in our bodies; they are not inert. Instead, trapped emotions and visceral fat are actually doing things to the body while they are present. Trapped emotions will bring on physical pain, emotional distress, or behavioral patterns that seem difficult to change. And visceral fat can cause a lot of inflammation in the body.

To process trapped emotions, Dr. Nelson recommends Muscle Testing, a simple communication method you do with your subconscious mind. If you are unfamiliar with muscle testing, here is a video of Dr. Nelson demonstrating how to do it with yourself or another person.   He also offers a free course to help you become more experienced using muscle testing for your wholeness journey.

Muscle testing is one of the awesome techniques that I use frequently. I'll ask myself a specific yes/no question and observe my body's physical response. Then, I can identify which emotions are trapped and where they are in my body.

One trapped emotion that I released through this technique was humiliation. In 7th grade, humiliation became trapped inside my body. My first six years of school were at a one-room schoolhouse, very much a "Little House on the Prairie" type of atmosphere. Starting in the 7th grade, though, we had to take the bus to the nearby town to attend school with many other children.

This was a big change because in my earlier school, there were only three students in my grade, but in 7th grade, there were over 30 students in my class alone. To help with this transition, a future classmate, the sister of one of my older sister's friends, invited me to a birthday party before school. At that party, we played Spin the Bottle, and I received my very first kiss.

Fast forward to the school year and to an all-school assembly. The main speaker was a magician. He was going through the crowd, asking questions, presumably writing the answer before the student answered it. I was one of the ones selected to answer a question. His question to me was, "Who gave you your first kiss?" It never occurred to me to make up a name, so I revealed the name of the person. I heard him groan from his seat behind me. I don't remember the details, but I know there was teasing afterward.

All these years, that sense of humiliation remained in me unconsciously until I released it with Emotional Code Techniques. It had become suppressed, which is even more dangerous than its effect on my conscious thought processes. I wonder what impact holding this emotion all those years really had on me. How did it filter the way I viewed situations? What good experiences did it prevent me from experiencing in life? How did it alter the way I viewed my world?

Here's another example: Let's say you feel discouraged from a past failure. You ask your body, "Do I have the trapped emotion of discouragement in my body?" Muscle test using the method that you prefer to receive the yes/no answer. Once identified, the emotions attached to these feelings can be released using a magnet or just an intention to let them go. What I've noticed is that, for me, there will be a wave of energy that balances and clears the trapped emotion.

Thus, the process is:

1. Sit in a comfortable chair such as a recliner or lie quietly on your bed or exercise mat.

2. Ask your body, "Do I have the trapped emotion of (fill in the blank) in my body that can be released today?

3. Perform a muscle test to pinpoint this trapped emotion. The book has a chart to drill down to the specific emotion. A free app in the app store can also guide you through the different emotions and how to identify them easily through muscle testing and a process of elimination.

4. Once the emotion is identified, ask if there is more you need to know about that emotion. This will be a yes/no answer provided by muscle testing. Sometimes, you might ask for an image of the situation that caused it and receive one. Otherwise, ask additional yes/no questions such as:

   ○ I feel discomfort in my whole leg. Is there a pinpoint area where this feeling started? (wait for an answer.)

   ○ Has this trapped emotion been here for six months or less? (Yes/no) The last year? (Yes/no) The last 5 years? (Yes/no) The last decade? (Yes/no)

   ○ Does it go back to when I was a child? (Yes/no)

   ○ Does it go back to when I was an infant? (Yes/no)

   ○ Does it go back to when I was in the womb? (Yes/no)

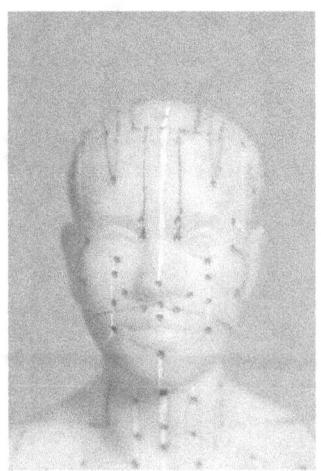

Many acupuncture meridians can be accessed on the head and face. Here, the Governing Vessel, shown in white extends down the middle of the head to the tip of the nose, under the middle of the bottom lip and down the middle of the throat.

Release the trapped emotion with intentionality and your words. "I release this trapped emotion of _____ from my body right now." You may also use a magnet to "dissolve it" with a swoop over it, much like a magnet erases a credit card. Any magnet will work for this, even a simple refrigerator magnet. The way to do this is to first locate the Governing Vessel meridian on the top of your head down to your neck. Take your magnet and trace this meridian, touching your skin, starting at your forehead and going down to your neck. The Governing Vessel meridian is shown in white on the picture.

The emotion releasing process shows that by following up with additional yes/no questions, you can pinpoint the exact location of the trapped emotion and even how long it has been there.

The answers you get will be instant and thus not really subject to being conjured up by your imagination. You'll know this is true because the truth feels different than a "lie" conjured up by your imagination. Many times, when the time frame of the trapped emotion was identified, I knew exactly what event caused the trapped emotion.

I'm always amazed at how emotions can even be trapped at a very young age. Using this technique, I uncovered the trapped emotion of insecurity that became trapped in my body at the age of two when our family moved to a new home! This became one of the earliest memories I have recovered.

After you release some of these trapped emotions, you'll start to feel so much freer that you will want to spend several more hours going through the process to see how much better you can feel overall.

How Trapped Emotions Act in the Body

In his book, Dr. Nelson emphasizes that everything is energy, and our bodies operate on this principle. Trapped emotions are like balls of energy that can distort the natural flow within the body. They cause disruptions that lead to pain or emotional imbalances.

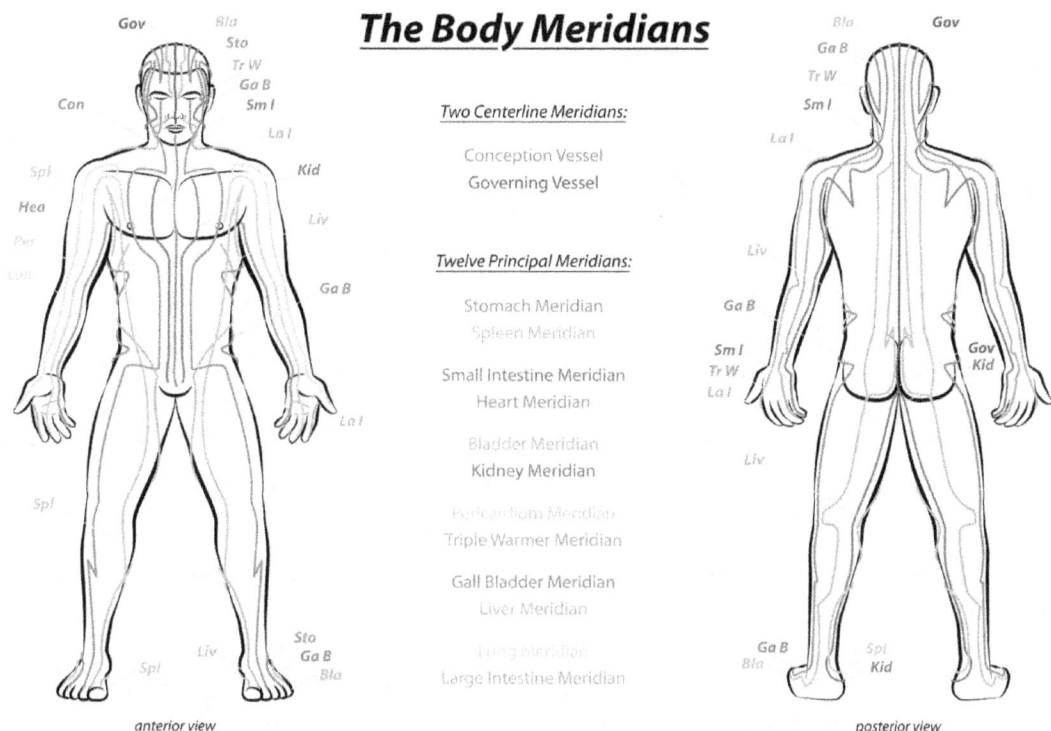

These pictures show the flow of all the meridians in the body. As you can see, all parts of your body are covered by these meridians. The Governing Vessel is also on the back of the body.

By releasing these trapped emotions, you restore the natural flow of energy, which results in improved health and well-being. This idea of trapped emotions interfering with health and wellness confirms the Chinese's ideas about their charts of the acupuncture meridians that flow through the body. They report that any blockages along these energy meridians are clearly related to disease.

The Emotion Code book provides detailed instructions on using muscle testing and magnets, making it accessible for those new to these concepts. It also includes stories and case studies illustrating the transformative effects of releasing trapped emotions, offering hope and inspiration.

Combining Trapped Emotion Identification and Release with Other Methods

Adding *The Emotion Code* principles into your Self-Healing Routine can be highly beneficial. To start the process, all you have to do is dedicate time to learning and practice muscle testing. Using this technique, you will understand these trapped emotions' origins. As you become more comfortable with the process, you can integrate it into your other regular practices, such as Meditation or Body Awareness Exercises.

For example, after a Body Scan, use Muscle Testing to explore any persistent areas of tension and discover if trapped emotions might be the cause. Dr. Nelson also encourages you to Journal your findings and progress, which can provide valuable insights and track your healing journey.

Teach Your Children This Method as Well

The beauty of what is taught in *The Emotion Code* is that it's simple, and anyone, even a child, can learn how to do it. What I like about it is that no advanced training or special equipment is needed to free yourself from trapped emotions. Following the straightforward steps outlined above and in the *The Emotion Code* book, you can clear the emotional baggage weighing you down, paving the way for a more balanced and vibrant life. This tool is a powerful addition to your healing repertoire, complementing other practices like Breathwork, Grounding Exercises, and Mindfulness, creating a holistic approach to well-being.

Another thing to remember is that no one is above having trapped emotions. They are found in those who tend to be emotional as well as those who seem to always have their emotions in check. If you have never done any emotional release techniques, you will have trapped emotions in your body. Start the hunt! Imagine the amount of light that children will carry in this world if they start this process at the age of 3 or 4.

The Emotion Code website provides access to certified Emotion Code healing practitioners to explore this further. You can find more info here: www.discoverhealing.com and by Googling, "Unlocking the Power of Emotion: How Emotion Code Practitioners Can Help You Find Emotional Freedom. A more direct URL is https://www.energyhealing.care/post/unlocking-the-power-of-emotion-how-emotion-code-practitioners-can-help-you-find-emotional-freedom

iAwake Technologies

Your brain operates on brainwaves, which are associated with different states of alertness. However, sometimes, due to prolonged stress, our brainwaves get "stuck" in one or more of these modes.

iAwake Technologies offers a fascinating approach to promoting healthy brainwave function using specialized audio tools. These tools are designed to stimulate your brain with specific frequencies, helping you achieve various states of consciousness, such as deep relaxation, focus, or heightened creativity.

The concept behind iAwake Technologies is rooted in the science of brainwave entrainment. Brainwave entrainment involves using rhythmic stimuli, like sound or light, to synchronize your brainwaves to a desired frequency.

When I first encountered iAwake Technologies, I was intrigued but unsure about what to expect. However, after adding their audio tracks into my daily routine, I noticed a significant improvement in my ability to manage stress and maintain a sense of calm. I also found I had greater clarity of thought.

iAwake Tool: Audio Tracks

One of my favorite tools from iAwake Technologies is its audio tracks for meditation. These tracks use a combination of binaural beats, isochronic tones, and other sound technologies to guide your brain into meditative states. Listening to these tracks makes it easier to quiet my mind and deepen my meditation practice. The soothing sounds and gentle rhythms help me let go of distractions and focus on the present moment. Over time, I've noticed that my ability to meditate has improved, even without audio assistance.

Listening to a track with a frequency that matches the brainwave patterns associated with deep relaxation can help you enter a relaxed state more quickly and easily. By doing this, it allows your nervous system, which may be stuck in sympathetic mode (fight-or-flight), to shift into parasympathetic mode (rest and digest). This technique leverages the brain's natural ability to sync with external rhythms, providing a powerful tool for enhancing mental and emotional well-being.

iAwake Technologies also focuses on personalization. They tailor a wide range of tracks to different needs, whether you want to improve sleep, enhance focus, or boost creativity. For example, their "Deep Delta" tracks are specifically designed to promote deep, restorative sleep by guiding your brain into delta wave patterns associated with the deepest stages of sleep. On nights when I struggle to fall asleep, these tracks have been a lifesaver, helping me drift off more quickly and wake up refreshed.

To incorporate these technologies into your daily routine, first identify your specific needs and goals. Are you seeking to reduce stress, improve focus, or enhance meditation? Once you have a clear idea of what you want to achieve, explore their library of audio tracks and choose those that align with your goals. Begin by setting aside dedicated time each day to listen to the tracks, whether during your morning meditation, a midday break, or before bed. Consistency is key, so try to make this a regular routine.

Combine iAwake Technologies with Other Practices

Combining iAwake Technologies with other self-healing practices can amplify their benefits. For example, you might listen to a relaxation track before or after practicing Breathwork or Grounding Exercises. Combining these tools can create a synergistic effect, enhancing your overall health.

Additionally, consider using iAwake tracks during moments of stress or anxiety. Listening to a calming track can help reset your mind and body, providing immediate relief and helping you regain your balance.

These tools can offer a practical and effective way to enhance your mental and emotional well-being. By integrating iAwake Technologies into your daily routine, you can harness the power of brainwave entrainment to support your journey toward greater health and resilience. Many free tracts on the website will allow you to experiment with some of this technology to see if it fits your overall health regimen. You can find them here www.iawaketechnology.com.

Summary

Numerous tools are available to support your self-healing journey. Whether you use Somatic Mapping, Resourcing, creating a Personal Healing Routine, Journaling, exploring "The Emotion Code," or using iAwake Technologies, each tool offers unique benefits that can enhance your well-being. They can also work synergistically with profound results.

Here are the summary tables for the somatic exercises in this chapter.

Tool/Exercise	Ease of Practice	Time Commitment
Somatic Mapping	Moderate	10–15 mins
Resourcing	Easy	5–10 mins
Personal Healing Routine	Moderate	Varies
Journaling	Easy	5–15 mins
The Emotion Code	Moderate	15–30 mins
iAwake Technologies	Easy	10–20 mins

Tool/Exercise	Enhances Body Awareness	Identifies Stored Emotions	Tracks Physical Sensations	Reduces Stress	Improves Self-Awareness
Somatic Mapping	✓	✓	✓	✓	✓
Resourcing				✓	✓
Personal Healing Routine	✓			✓	✓
Journaling		✓		✓	✓

Tool/Exercise	Enhances Body Awareness	Identifies Stored Emotions	Tracks Physical Sensations	Reduces Stress	Improves Self-Awareness
The Emotion Code	✓	✓	✓	✓	✓
iAwake Technologies				✓	✓

In the next chapter, we'll discuss the holistic healing framework that helps you really understand how the body, mind and spirit are truly entwined.

Chapter 8

INTEGRATING MIND, BODY, AND SPIRIT

The body is the instrument through which the soul expresses itself.

-- *SAINT THOMAS AQUINAS*

HAVE YOU EVER FELT beautiful calmness when you watched an extraordinary sunset? Or, during a walk, have you intentionally noticed nature around you and been amazed by it? In these moments, we integrate every aspect of our being—mind, body, and spirit—into our healing process. This chapter explores how holistic healing can bring those elements together, fostering a sense of balance and well-being.

The Holistic Healing Framework

Holistic healing is a powerful approach that acknowledges the interconnectedness of mind, body, and spirit. This concept recognizes that our mental, physical, and spiritual health are deeply entwined, and to achieve true well-being, we must address all these facets. Holistic healing considers the whole person, not just symptoms or isolated issues. By doing so, it offers a comprehensive path to health that goes beyond conventional treatments.

The importance of holistic healing in Somatic Therapy is great. When we ignore one aspect of our being, we create imbalances that can manifest as stress, illness, or emotional turmoil. For example, persistent stress can lead to physical ailments like headaches or digestive issues, while unresolved emotional pain can impact our spiritual well-being. By embracing a holistic approach, we can address these imbalances and promote overall harmony within ourselves.

A holistic healing framework is composed of mental, physical, and spiritual health practices. Mental health practices such as Mindfulness, Meditation, and Emotional Regulation are fundamental. These practices help us become more aware of our thoughts and emotions, allowing us to manage them effectively.

Mindfulness, for example, involves paying attention to the present moment without judgment. This simple practice can reduce stress, improve focus, and enhance mental strength. These benefits occur as we learn to control our emotions effectively.

You might be asking, "How does this really work? Is it really possible?" Scientists have actually studied this! Mindfulness encourages observing thoughts and emotions without judgment, reducing the likelihood of overreacting to stressors. This helps prevent the "fight-or-flight" response from being unnecessarily triggered. Regular mindfulness practices have been shown to lower cortisol, the hormone associated with stress, leading to a calmer physiological state. Mindfulness builds emotional resilience, allowing individuals to better handle challenging situations and recover more quickly from stress.

And what about improving focus? Does that work according to the scientists? Yes! Mindfulness has been found to strengthen the brain's prefrontal cortex, which is responsible for focus, planning, and decision-making. This improves the ability to concentrate and filter out distractions. By bringing attention back to the present moment, Mindfulness minimizes mind-wandering, a common source of distraction and reduced productivity. Mindfulness cultivates a heightened awareness of one's surroundings and tasks, improving the ability to stay engaged and attentive.

This practice rewires the brain over time, improving sustained attention and the ability to refocus after distractions. Integrating mindfulness into daily activities, like Mindful Eating or Mindful Walking, trains the mind to stay present even during routine tasks.

Mindfulness also changes your relationship with thoughts and emotions. It helps you view your thoughts as transient mental events rather than absolute truths, reducing their emotional impact. By focusing on the present, mindfulness interrupts rumination and worry, which are significant contributors to stress.

Mindfulness practices like deep breathing encourage the "rest-and-digest" response, reducing physical and emotional tension. Focusing on the present reduces the mental clutter caused by excessive multitasking or future-oriented thinking, fostering a sense of calm.

By practicing nonjudgmental observation, individuals gain better control over impulsive reactions, leading to more measured responses. It increases emotional awareness, making it easier to identify and address emotions before they escalate.

Meditation

Meditation provides a space for reflection and inner peace, helping us connect with our deeper selves. Scripture tells us that the Kingdom of God is within. Meditating helps us develop this inner kingdom so that navigating in the physical world is accomplished with more success and handled with more ease. In stillness, we become more attuned to divine guidance, allowing us to align our actions with a higher purpose.

This practice fosters clarity, resilience, and gratitude, enabling us to approach life's challenges with a spirit of faith and grace. Through meditation, we cultivate the inner strength and wisdom needed to shine our light in the world.

Physical health practices are equally vital. Exercise, Nutrition, and Somatic Exercises form the bedrock of this component. Regular physical activity, whether a brisk walk, yoga, or strength training, boosts our mood, increases energy levels, and supports overall health. Nutrition plays a crucial role as well. A balanced diet rich in whole foods, vegetables, fruits, and healthy proteins and fats nourishes our bodies and fuels our minds so they can operate at an optimal level.

Somatic Exercises, which focus on body awareness and movement, help release tension and promote relaxation, bridging the gap between mental and physical health. They allow us to be the best we can be in non-stressful and stressful situations.

Spiritual health practices add another layer to the holistic framework. These practices revolve around spirituality, purpose, and connection. Spirituality doesn't necessarily mean religion; it's about finding meaning and connection. Practices like Prayer, Contemplation, or Time in Nature can enhance our sense of purpose and comfort us during challenging times. Connecting with something larger than ourselves, whether a higher power, nature, or a community, fosters a sense of belonging and support.

Creating a balanced healing plan involves:

- Assessing individual needs and goals

- Allocating time for mental, physical, and spiritual practices

- Adjusting the plan based on feedback and progress

How to Assess What You Need to Balance Body, Mind, and Spirit

To start or enhance your current holistic journey, you will need to know the baseline of where you are at this moment.

What areas of your life need attention? Are you struggling with stress, not getting enough physical activity, or are you feeling disconnected spiritually from your Creator or other humans? Once you've identified your needs, it's time to set realistic goals and allocate time for each practice.

For example, you could dedicate some time in the morning to Mindfulness Meditation, about 40 minutes in the afternoon to Physical Exercise, and 30 minutes in the evenings to spiritual practices like Journaling or spending Time in Nature.

Adjusting your plan as you go along is a given. Healing is rarely linear, and what works today might need tweaking tomorrow. What works is to check in with yourself regularly to see how you're progressing and be open to making changes. If a particular practice isn't resonating with you, try something different. Every technique won't work for everyone. Remember, the goal is to create a sustainable routine that supports your lifestyle and journey to wholeness. Be gentle with yourself, you are possibly learning an entirely new way of functioning. Some days may feel like one step forward or two steps back. Give yourself grace to begin anew each day if you have a setback.

To illustrate the power of holistic healing, I want to tell you about Lisa, who had a big battle with recovering from trauma. She decided to use this type of holistic approach for her recovery.

Lisa initially felt disconnected from herself. She felt emotionally flat in all circumstances as if her ability to feel anything had been completely broken. She struggled with anxiety and depression. She started practicing Mindfulness Meditation in her daily routine. This helped her manage her anxiety, and she started feeling a little empowered.

Next, she began a Gentle Exercise regimen and improved her diet, focusing on nourishing her body with whole foods. When she did both of these together, she convinced herself to continue them by asking herself how she could do the exercise if she didn't improve her diet. They were inseparable.

Additionally, Lisa found solace in spiritual practices like Journaling and Nature walks. She would walk in parks near her home and nearby forests and occasionally drive to the mountains or ocean to spend some time alone. Over time, she noticed a significant improvement in her mental, physical, and spiritual health, demonstrating the transformative power of a holistic approach.

What Does A Balanced Daily Routine Look Like?

An example of how to have a balanced daily routine is below:

1. Start the day with a few minutes of Mindfulness Meditation to set a positive tone.

2. Follow it with a nutritious breakfast high in protein and healthy fats and lower in carbohydrates.

3. Mid-morning, engage in physical activity, like stretching or a brisk walk.

4. In the afternoon, take time for a Somatic Exercise or Body Scan to release any tension.

5. As the day winds down, spend time in Nature or engage in a Spiritual Practice that resonates with you, like Journaling or Prayer.

6. End the day with a healthy dinner and a few moments of Reflection and gratitude.

If you ask around, you will easily start accumulating testimonials from individuals who have embraced holistic healing. These testimonials further underscore its benefits. One person shared how integrating Mindfulness, Regular Exercise, and Spiritual Practices helped them overcome chronic stress and find inner peace. He mentioned that he had been ignoring Spiritual Practices, but they were the missing piece in his health puzzle.

A woman mentioned to me that a balanced diet and Somatic Exercises significantly reduced her anxiety and improved her overall quality of life; before doing these exercises, her emotions completely controlled her day. If good things happened in one moment, her emotions would be very excited and positive, but if a stressful situation arose, then her emotions would plummet into anxiety and depression. This made each day feel like an uncontrollable rollercoaster ride. She was exhausted from the ups and downs that filled each day and was desperate for relief.

It didn't take long for the nutritional changes to start making a difference. In about a week her moods started stabilizing just from keeping blood sugar levels stable. Then she added Somatic Exercises and was able to control even more of her anxiety. Now, she only experiences anxiety once every few months and hopes that, over time, this will be totally gone.

These stories reflect the profound impact that a holistic approach can have, offering a path to healing that is both comprehensive and deeply personal. Life is fuller when all aspects of yourself—mind, body, and spirit—are covered and operating at a high level.

Holistic healing addresses the interconnectedness of mind, body, and spirit. Integrating mental, physical, and spiritual practices into our daily lives can create a balanced routine that promotes well-being. You may be wondering what exactly this type of well-being looks like.

Physically – You develop an exercise routine that works for you. You choose to eat healthy foods and give your body the nourishment it needs. When you eat meals, you are mindful of every bite and how it nourishes you. Your newfound knowledge of listening to your body's signals has given you confidence and helped you manage each day's eating habits with greater insight, and you can't wait to get your exercise in for the day. Movement makes you feel great.

Mentally – You are in control of your thoughts and emotions. You have learned to take every thought captive and say no to the negative recordings that used to play continually throughout the day. You control your emotions rather than allowing them to control you.

Spiritually – You have gained greater insight into what it means to be more spiritually connected. You acknowledge that you have a spirit and that it is always connected to the Creator of all things. You have learned to accept this divine unconditional love and allow it to strengthen you each day.

Whether you're struggling with stress, physical ailments, or a sense of disconnection, holistic healing offers a path to harmony and health. What would your life be like once you have all three of these areas operating at a high level? Can you envision it yet?

Spiritual Practices to Enhance Somatic Therapy

The role of spirituality in healing is profound and multifaceted. In its most basic form, spirituality is the search for meaning and connection beyond the tangible world. It's about finding a sense of purpose and belonging. And if you keep searching for deeper spirituality, that sense of purpose and belonging will have a God component.

When you have a more profound connection to something larger than yourself, that's when you can experience immense comfort and resilience, especially during challenging times. Here's an example, but you decide… When you have had a God experience or an experience that filled you with so much awe that you cannot deny God exists, there's an immense sense of comfort that settles into your heart. Your whole perspective on life changes without you trying to change it. You stop rationalizing about what happened and accept it. You make room for God.

If this is difficult for you at first, and if your beliefs and feelings toward God are negative, you can start by praying a short prayer. Just simply pray, "God if you are real and true and if it's true that You have unconditional love for me, will You show me in a way that I will know beyond a shadow of a doubt that it is You?" In my experience, this is a prayer that the Creator never fails to answer.

Some people have to work up to this point slowly. They have to appreciate Nature first, then one day, they have an AWE experience that is undeniable and life changing. Then these awe experiences continue until they have an actual encounter with God. These encounters with God never happen if someone isn't looking for them.

The "science of awe" is now a recognized field of study, with research appearing in medical literature and scientists publishing popular books on the topic. Awe is quickly entering the mainstream! Some psychologists are even dedicating their careers to exploring this phenomenon, as experiencing awe has been shown to significantly impact and transform people's lives.

You won't read about this in very many books on Somatic Therapy, and you won't hear about it in talk therapy either. Certain professions have based their entire philosophy on being anti-God. Some professions even go so far as to call those who believe "crazy" or "deluded," but to those who have gone through the process of finding God in their spirituality, these professionals only look like they are misguided.

Spirituality Should Not Be Mechanical

Spirituality can be mechanical, such as going to church or doing yoga in a ritualistic manner, or it can be transforming. When it's transformative, it positively impacts mental health by fostering hope, compassion, and inner peace because we know we have experienced grace on some level and are well cared for. When transformative experiences happen, we begin to see our whole life as a continuum of experiences that taught us certain truths that led up to the position we are in right now.

Many people are familiar with what happens to those diagnosed with cancer: they begin to reflect on their life and ask the question, "What was my life all about, and what was its purpose?" These people start seeking spiritual answers; unless someone is seeking it, they will not find it. The type of spirituality they are seeking is not mechanical or ritualistic. It's the deep sense of spirituality they are looking for. Cancer patients are more likely to have moments of revelation and awe that change their lives, sometimes leading to miraculous healings.

Amplifying Healing with Spiritual Practices

When integrated with Somatic Therapy, spiritual practices can amplify the healing process, offering a holistic approach that nurtures the mind, body, and spirit. The point is that leaving God out of the picture is only operating in two of the three parts of yourself.

Specific spiritual practices can significantly enhance Somatic Therapy. One such practice is Meditation and Mindfulness. Meditation can involve reading scriptures in the Bible, reflecting on something that happened to you, or focusing on an emotion. In Eastern religions, meditation is clearing out extraneous thoughts that distract the mind. When you meditate, you direct your attention to one thing. This process makes connecting with your inner self easier.

Mindfulness Meditation involves focusing on the present moment without judgment. This isn't a bad idea at all, because judging situations or people is something that can harm us. Have you ever noticed that judging a friend is a good way to distance yourself from that person?

Focusing on the present moment can mean paying attention to your breath or observing your thoughts and emotions without getting caught up in them. It could also mean observing and identifying your thoughts and emotions and then making a decision on what to do with them——keep them or give them away to a God who will gladly take them to transform your heart.

You could also see your thoughts as clouds passing by. Just observe them as they move past you, then let them go on by without taking ownership of them. When you do Mindfulness Meditation, you will notice your mind is calmed, and you feel a sense of spiritual grounding. You feel more centered and connected.

Prayer and Contemplation

Prayer and Contemplation are other powerful spiritual practices. Prayer is a way to connect to God that extends beyond the boundaries of time and space. Yet, it gives you a sense of instant connection and comfort. Prayer is a way to seek guidance, express gratitude, or find solace in stressful times.

Conversely, Contemplation involves spending time in quiet thought, reflecting on life's deeper meanings and your place within them. Both practices create a spiritual anchor, helping you navigate life's challenges more easily. They also help you begin to get an answer for the question that most humans have at some point… "Why am I here, and why now at this point in time? What is my purpose, and am I accomplishing what I am supposed to?"

Rituals and Ceremonies

Rituals and ceremonies also play a significant role in spiritual healing. Creating meaningful rituals can bring a sense of structure and purpose to your spiritual practice. These rituals don't have to be elaborate; they can be as simple as lighting a candle, saying a daily affirmation, or performing a small act of kindness. They're good to get you started on the spiritual path, but seeking your direct connection to God goes far beyond the benefits of rituals and ceremonies. Still, these practices are important because they essentially set up memories of times you spent in pursuit of God.

Celebrating by having a ceremony marks a challenging period's end or times when you achieved a personal milestone. These times provide a sense of closure and renewal. These practices create a sacred space for healing, allowing you to honor your journey and the progress you've made. And here's a tip that you won't read in other books: there are two types of ceremonies: 1) the type that you initiate and 2) the type that God inspires you to do. It's always the latter one that is going to be more transformative.

Integrating spirituality into your daily life is transformative. Not only does it have the power to change your physical and mental health, but it can also start to reverse the clock and make you look much younger. Only through a spiritual connection to God can the "peace that passes understanding" be achieved. This peace replaces the worry and stress that can age us beyond our biological years.

Some Ideas to Get Started

Carve out time in your schedule for a morning meditation or prayer to set a positive tone for the day. You could sit still waiting to hear from God during this time. You can ask, "God, what is on your heart today?" or "God, what do you believe about me?" Then, when the thought enters your mind, you will know it is from God if it is beyond your own thinking.

There is a tip here that you should know: sometimes God will 'test' you to see how long you will wait for him to give you a message. This may be why the Quakers actually don't go to hear a sermon; they go to hear what God has to tell them for the day. So don't give up too early while you are waiting.

Even taking just a few minutes to connect with your inner self in the morning can significantly affect how you approach your day. Imagine how blessed you will feel if you know that every morning, you aren't starting your day until you get the word for the day. What would you be like after 30 days of doing this? How much healthier and connected would you feel?

Integrating daily Mindfulness practices, like taking a Mindful Walk, practicing Gratitude, or engaging in Deep Breathing exercises, can help you feel grounded and present. But by adding God to the process, you can count on transformation.

Creating a sacred space in your home for rituals and reflection can also be beneficial. This space can be a small corner with meaningful objects, like a candle, a journal, or something from nature that is a momentum of a specific awe moment in time. A dedicated space for spiritual practices is instrumental to maintaining a routine and provides a sanctuary for reflection and healing. And it's biblical, as well.

The impact of spirituality on healing is profound. It is the most critical leg of the mind, body, and spirit healing journey. Being strong in spirit and connected firmly to the God of all creation is the true foundation of wholeness. It is my hope that this book can be used as a bridge between an area that traditional churches have not embraced and bring in this holistic approach to healing.

Spirituality fosters greater emotional stability, helping you bounce back from setbacks and maintain a positive outlook. When you are confused about which way to go in your life, and you receive an answer from God on it, this divine interaction eliminates all the anxiety you had previously. When God tells you why a particular relationship ended, there's no more need for depression. You can move forward.

Spirituality is a Subject That Has Been Studied

Studies have shown that individuals who engage in regular spiritual practices experience improved mental and physical health outcomes—and it's no wonder that this is true. People who pray have lower stress and anxiety levels, better emotional regulation, and a stronger sense of well-being. They know who they are and don't feel like they are tossed around like a leaf in the wind.

Developing spiritual practices into Somatic Therapy creates a powerful synergy that nurtures the whole person. By embracing these practices, you can cultivate a more profound sense of inner peace, resilience, and well-being.

Nutrition and Lifestyle: Supporting Your Healing Journey

The role of nutrition in healing can be exceptionally profound. What you eat fuels your body and influences your mental, emotional, and physical health. The connection between diet and mental health is well-documented. Your brain needs a constant supply of nutrients to function optimally. High-quality foods rich in vitamins, minerals, and antioxidants nourish your brain and protect it from oxidative stress.

On the flip side, diets high in refined sugars and processed/ultra-processed foods can impair brain function, leading to mood disorders like depression and anxiety. One study from the 1970s found that those patients in a mental institution experienced every type of mental disorder as a group when they went through blood sugar highs and lows. These are times when your brain can't rationally think straight.

If you have ever read crime reports for fun, you will find quite a few where someone committed a crime because they were hungry. One example I recall is of a young man who broke the window of a store to get donuts he needed to raise his low blood sugar levels! Sugary foods are devoid of B vitamins and minerals, the very nutrients you need to think critically, make good decisions, and be happy. As he stuffed the donuts in his mouth, the police pulled up to arrest him.

A nutrient-rich diet has far-reaching benefits, including improved energy levels, mood, and general physical health. When your body receives the right nutrients, it operates more efficiently, making you feel more energetic and emotionally balanced. What many people don't realize is that eating a nutrient-rich diet also seems to open up a channel to hear God directly.

Certain nutrients are particularly beneficial for mental and physical health. Omega-3 fatty acids in foods like salmon, walnuts, and flaxseeds are essential for brain health. They help reduce inflammation and improve cognitive function. However, many nutrients are needed for brain health: all the B vitamins, protein, magnesium, boron, iodine, vitamin E, vitamin C, selenium, phosphorus, and more.

Besides vitamins and minerals, medicinal constituents of foods such as the antioxidants of green tea, the anthocyanidins abundant in berries, dark chocolate, and leafy greens, and other compounds also play a crucial role. They combat oxidative stress and inflammation, which can worsen mental health issues.

Eating whole foods, which are unprocessed and natural, is equally important. This isn't to say you should eat everything raw. Grains must be soaked, sprouted, and cooked to neutralize harmful ingredients such as phytates and oxalates. Foods provide a range of nutrients that work together to support your body's systems. Unlike processed foods, which often lack essential nutrients and are high in harmful additives, chemicals, and heavy metals, whole foods offer the best of nature's bounty.

Creating a healing diet involves planning balanced meals that incorporate a variety of fruits, vegetables, nuts, seeds, healthy proteins, and healthy fats. One way to change your diet if you aren't consuming some of these plants is to fill half your plate with colorful vegetables and fruits. These foods are packed with vitamins, minerals, and antioxidants that support every aspect of your health. Then add a healthy protein like pasture-raised chicken, grass-fed beef, low mercury fish, dairy protein, beans, legumes, or tofu to the mix. Proteins are the building blocks of your body, aiding in tissue repair and growth.

Healthy fats in avocados, nuts, fatty fish, and olive oil should also be part of your diet. These fats are essential for brain health and help you feel satiated. Add a few tablespoons of these healthy fats to your diet daily. Avoid hydrogenated fats, oils such as corn, canola, safflower, sunflower, vegetable oil, processed foods, and sugars, which all can trigger inflammation and negatively impact your mood and energy levels.

Hydration

Hydration can be considered part of your nutrition and is another critical aspect of a healthy lifestyle. Drinking enough water is essential for maintaining bodily functions, from digestion to circulation. Dehydration can lead to fatigue, headaches, and decreased mental clarity. Aim to drink at least eight glasses of water daily, more if you're active or live in a hot climate. Carry a glass or stainless steel water bottle and take sips throughout the day to stay hydrated.

Don't Forget Exercise

Lifestyle practices are just as important as nutrition in supporting your healing journey. Regular physical activity is a cornerstone of good health. Exercise releases endorphins, the body's natural mood lifters, and helps reduce stress. It also improves cardiovascular health, strengthens muscles, and boosts overall energy levels.

If you're not exercising now, begin slowly and aim for at least 30 minutes of moderate exercise at least three days of the week. This could be anything from a brisk walk to a stretching or dance class. The key is to find activities you enjoy, which will make it easier to stick with them.

But if you have a serious chronic disease, start out in a small way. Too much exercise could generate a lot of excessive free radicals that aggravate your condition. Get your doctor's approval before you sign up for a health club's strenuous programs.

Combine Nutrition with Other Techniques

Combining nutrition with stress management techniques can further enhance your well-being. Mindfulness, Meditation, and Deep Breathing magnifies how you manage stress effectively. When combined with a balanced diet, these practices create a powerful synergy that supports your mental and physical health.

For instance, Mindful Eating, which is paying full attention to the experience of eating and drinking, can help you make healthier food choices and enjoy your meals more fully. It encourages you to listen to your body's hunger and fullness cues, preventing overeating and promoting a healthier relationship with food.

Daily practice of these exercises can create a holistic approach to health and wellness. Each element is crucial in your healing journey, whether focusing on Nutrition, Exercise,

Hydration, or Stress Management. By paying attention to what you eat, staying active, keeping hydrated, and managing stress, you can create a balanced lifestyle that nurtures your mind, body, and spirit.

Sleep and Rest: The Foundation of Healing

Sleep is often the unsung hero in our wellness toolkit. You may change your nutrition and movement and resolve your traumatic events from the past, but if you aren't on a healthy sleep schedule, your body is still in chaos. Adequate sleep is a cornerstone for mental health, providing a reset for our minds and bodies.

Sleep helps you process emotions, consolidate memories, and clear out toxins that build up during the day. This cleansing process occurs during sleep (combined with not eating for 12 hours of the day) is called autophagy. It is essential for maintaining mental clarity and emotional regulation.

Without enough sleep, you're more likely to feel overwhelmed, anxious, and irritable. Sleep deprivation is known to impair cognitive functions like decision-making and problem-solving, making it harder to cope with daily stressors. It also makes you accident-prone.

Sleep plays a critical role in physical recovery and immune function. Have you ever noticed that you rapidly begin to slow down when you get a cold, flu, or other infection? Even on the first day of the infection, you sleep longer, and even during hours you don't usually sleep. This is a natural body reaction and shouldn't be dismissed.

During deep sleep, your body goes into repair mode, healing muscles, tissues, and cells. This is when your immune system gets revved up and growth hormone is released, aiding tissue regeneration and muscle growth. If you're not getting sufficient rest, your body can't effectively carry out these repair processes, leaving you more susceptible to injury and illness.

A lack of sleep weakens the immune response, making you more vulnerable to infections and prolonging recovery times. Quality sleep provides the foundation for a robust immune system, enabling your body to fend off illnesses and recover more quickly when you get sick.

But how does sleep improve emotional regulation? Adequate rest helps stabilize mood and emotional responses. When you're well-rested, you're better equipped to handle stress and emotional challenges. You won't react to every little irritant that appears before you because your brain can discern the difference between what matters and what doesn't matter. Sleep acts as a buffer, reducing the intensity of negative emotions and helping you maintain a balanced perspective.

On the flip side, sleep deprivation can amplify emotional reactions, making you more prone to mood swings and emotional outbursts. And, of course, having a day of emotional ups and downs is a day where you won't get much done except for flustering those who happen to be in your pathway.

What It Means to Prioritize Sleep

By prioritizing sleep for your health, you create a stable emotional environment that supports overall mental health and resilience. Prioritizing sleep means you are on a sleep schedule, one that gets you in bed and asleep, preferably by 11 p.m., so that the beauty hormone called human growth hormone can be released in a high dose between midnight and 3 a.m. This hormone is closely linked to all the different sleep stages.

Prioritizing sleep also includes altering what you eat and drink a few hours before bed and making your bedroom a sleep haven. And there's one more aspect of prioritizing sleep that some people often forget—the part about getting their minds free of thoughts and feelings that will keep them overanalyzing everything (rumination).

How to Set Up Your Bedroom as a Sleep Haven

With all the data we now have from toxicologists, environmental scientists, building biologists, and radiation specialists, you can easily create a sleep-friendly environment to get the rest you need.

Here are the recommendations you need to start this process. You do not have to do these steps in order and can choose whichever ones are easiest first.

1. Invest in a good mattress. Ensure that the materials used to make the mattress and pillows are not saturated with flame retardants, which have been linked with chronic fatigue syndrome. Flame retardants are full of PFAS, those forever chemicals that have been in the news so much in the last few years. The best mattresses are ones made from natural fibers such as cotton, latex, and wool. These mattresses are more costly, but they are a lifetime investment.

2. Make sure that your pillow matches your cervical curvature. This is where your chiropractor can help you make this decision. The cervical curve of a 5-foot-tall 90-pound woman differs greatly from a 6'3" man who weighs 285 pounds. Not getting the cervical curve right will lead to headaches and tension in the head, neck, and shoulders and result in greater levels of anxiety.

3. Consider getting blackout curtains. They will ensure that your room stays cool and dark.

4. Get your home checked for dirty electricity. A building biologist is the correct professional for this job and checks for high-voltage transients that travel through your home's electrical system. These transients can create free radicals in your body from their electromagnetic fields as far as six feet from the electrical cords and outlets in your home. Free radicals will disrupt your cellular function throughout your body when you don't

have enough antioxidants to counter them.

Dirty electricity is usually found wherever dimmer switches are used to dim lights and when a home's electrical system is not up to code.

Get your phone charging system out of your bedroom. Keep your phone out of your bedroom at night, no matter what. It's tempting to believe that you have to have the phone near you just in case a family member needs you, but this may be where you can step out in faith and ask for divine support to alert you if you are needed.

The alternative is that you expose yourself to the harmful effects of electromagnetic radiation that negatively affect your cells. You cannot "will" these effects away; denying them doesn't stop them either.

Phones give off electromagnetic radiation because they pulsate constantly. You might want to check out Gauss or electrosmog meters online at Amazon to see how different rooms in your home measure up. One reasonably priced meter is the Cornet Electrosmog Meter, which tests your location for Gauss, radiofrequency, and low-frequency pollution.

Exposure to electromagnetic fields from cell phones has been linked with cellular stress, immune dysfunction, and dysregulation of calcium metabolism. If you're human, these effects will eventually catch up with you, whether you feel them or not.

6. Remove computers, tablets, and any other devices in your bedroom that emit blue light or contain screens. The blue light emitted by phones, tablets, and computers disrupts your body's natural sleep-wake cycle by suppressing melatonin production. Turn off screens at least an hour before bedtime and engage in relaxing activities like reading a book or listening to calming music.

7. You may feel you need sleep aids to fall asleep. This is where you can use calming sounds and scents to enhance your sleep environment. Use essential oils, not products on the market that contain paraffin or the word "fragrance" on their labels. Fragrance is a term that is always linked to unknown chemicals put together and added to a product. They are considered the most pervasive source of toxins in our homes today. Fragrance equals phthalates, which are hormone disruptors.

Fragrance chemicals bind to dust in your home and remain in the air unless you physically purify it. Thus, you are re-exposed to them 24/7. Fragrances are part of the reason why, in 2018, 42% of people in the U.S. were diagnosed with asthma.

Studies have found that scented paraffin candles are a big problem. When you light the candle, you put toxins into the air, liberating benzene, toluene, formaldehyde, and ultrafine particles (particles that are <0.1 mm that directly enter your brain past the blood-brain-barrier and have been found down in the deepest parts of the lungs in the alveoli where gas exchange occurs. These particles are then circulated to all your organs. Incense is worse! Essential oils are completely different. Your body can handle essential oils, and their ingredients are medicinal and not harmful. Essential oils like lavender and chamomile have soothing properties that promote relaxation and improve sleep quality. Consider using a diffuser or pillow spray to infuse your bedroom with these calming scents.

8. White noise machines or apps can also be helpful, masking background noises that might disturb your sleep. Consistency is vital, so establish a bedtime routine that signals it's time to wind down.

Improving sleep quality requires a combination of all these techniques. Certainly, establishing a regular sleep schedule is very effective, but if you don't give up the cell phone and subject yourself to the electromagnetic fields from cell phones, you will be destroying the good effects of a regular sleep schedule.

Regular Sleep Schedule

A regular sleep schedule depends on you going to bed and waking up at the same time every day, even on weekends. This consistency helps regulate your body's internal clock and its circadian rhythms, making it easier to fall asleep and wake up naturally. You'll feel much more grounded and balanced when your circadian rhythms are spot-on. Consider how you feel when you travel across different time zones—this is an example of what happens to the body when the circadian rhythms are disrupted.

Other Tips for Better Sleep

There are additional methods that may be exactly what you need to create a sleep haven in your bedroom. These methods address what you can physically do to enhance your sleep by working in the body realm.

1. Practicing Relaxation techniques before bed can also make a significant difference. Deep Breathing, Progressive Muscle Relaxation, and Gentle Stretching calm your nervous system and prepare your body for sleep. The calming occurs because your body switches out of fight-or-flight and enters parasympathetic functions.

2. Practicing Mindfulness and Meditation for relaxation can also be beneficial. These practices help you stay present and reduce stress, creating a sense of calm that carries over into your sleep.

Consuming foods high in the amino acid tryptophan have also been linked to better sleep. Your body converts tryptophan into serotonin that can help improve mood, and melatonin, which promotes sleep.

The estimated requirement for tryptophan for adults is 4 to 5 mg tryptophan per kilogram body weight. For a 154-pound adult who weighs 70 kilograms, this amount is 280-350 mg per day. Check out the table below on how easy it is to get more of this amino acid in your diet daily.

Table 1. Foods and Their Tryptophan Content

Food	Tryptophan Content
Eggs, 1 large	83 mg
Tuna (canned white), lobster, snapper, 3 oz.	248–252 mg
Beef roast, pork roast, 3 oz.	229–238 mg
Turkey (light meat), 3 oz.	214 mg
Crab, salmon, tilapia, 3 oz.	192–231 mg
Tofu, ½ cup	296 mg
Soybeans (edamame), 1 cup	270 mg
Cheddar cheese, Mozzarella cheese, 1 oz.	90–146 mg
Whole milk, 2% milk, 1 cup	107–120 mg
Yogurt (low fat), 8 oz.	68 mg
Oats, 1 cup	147 mg
Buckwheat (groats), 1 cup	82 mg
Pumpkin and squash seeds, 1 oz.	163 mg
Almonds, peanuts, pistachios, cashews, black walnuts, 1 oz.	60–90 g

3. Avoiding caffeine in any form (coffee, caffeinated drinks, chocolate) is extremely helpful. Caffeine revs up your nervous system, giving you plenty of energy so you won't want to go to sleep. Caffeine can stay in your system for hours, disrupting your ability to fall asleep. Experts often recommend stopping any caffeine intake by 3 p.m. each day.

But how much is too much? The answer varies per person. Some people will experience side effects such as heart palpitations, anxiety, increased blood pressure, increased heart rate, and insomnia with an intake of less than 400 mg per day. And one study showed that pregnant women may consume 3000 mg of caffeine safely per day. Check out this chart of the amount of caffeine in commonly consumed foods.

Table 2. Foods and Their Caffeine Content

Food	Caffeine Content
Standard Coffee, 8 oz.	100 mg
Starbucks Grande Vanilla Latte, Grande Blonde Roast, 16 oz.	170–360 mg
Starbucks Grande hot chocolate, 16 oz.	25 mg
Swiss Miss hot chocolate, Nestle hot chocolate, 16 oz.	0 mg
Decaffeinated coffee, 1 cup	1–50 mg
Milk chocolate (33% cocoa), 3.5 oz.	45 mg
Bittersweet chocolate (55% cocoa), 3.5 oz.	124 mg
Cocoa chocolate (100% cocoa), 3.5 oz.	240 mg
Green tea, 1 cup	30–50 mg
Yerba mate tea, 1 cup	20–180 mg
Caffeinated chewing gum, 2 pieces	50 mg
Energy drinks, 8 oz.	50–505 mg
Red Bull energy drink, 8.4 oz.	80 mg

4. How much you eat also affects your sleep, especially if you eat a heavy meal later in the evening. Heavy meals can lead to discomfort and indigestion, making it more difficult to get restful sleep.

5. Taking short breaks throughout the day can help you recharge and maintain focus. A five-minute pause to stretch, breathe deeply, step outside for fresh air, or put your feet in the grass for 10 minutes can make a huge difference.

6. Daily exercise and being in nature also facilitate a better night of sleep.

7. Scheduling regular periods of rest and self-care is essential. Whether it's a weekend afternoon nap or a quiet evening with a good book, permitting yourself to rest can rejuvenate your mind and body.

Summary

As you weave together the practices of holistic healing, spirituality, nutrition, exercise, and rest, you create a balanced and nurturing environment for your journey toward wholeness. Each element supports the others, forming a cohesive approach to health that addresses the mind, body, and spirit.

Practice	Ease of Practice	Time Commitment
Mindfulness	Easy	10–15 mins
Meditation	Moderate	10–30 mins
Nutrition	Moderate	Varies
Somatic Exercises	Moderate	10–20 mins
Spiritual Practices	Easy	15–30 mins
Daily Routine Practices	Moderate	Varies
Prayer	Easy	5 mins
Contemplation	Easy	10 mins
Rituals	Easy	Varies
Awe Experiences	Moderate	Varies
Balanced Meals	Moderate	Varies
Hydration	Easy	5 mins
Exercise	Moderate	30 mins
Mindful Eating	Easy	Varies
Daily Breaks/Rest	Easy	5–10 mins

Practice	Reduces Stress	Improves Focus	Enhances Emotional Resilience	Supports Overall Well-Being
Mindfulness	✓	✓	✓	✓
Meditation	✓	✓	✓	✓
Nutrition	✓			✓
Somatic Exercises	✓		✓	✓
Spiritual Practices	✓		✓	✓

Practice	Reduces Stress	Improves Focus	Enhances Emotional Resilience	Supports Overall Well-Being
Mindfulness Meditation (Morning)	✓	✓	✓	✓
Nutritious Breakfast	✓	✓		
Physical Activity (Morning Stretch/Walk)	✓	✓		✓
Somatic Exercises/Body Scan	✓		✓	✓
Spiritual Practice (Evening Journaling/Prayer)	✓	✓	✓	✓

Practice	Reduces Stress	Improves Focus	Enhances Emotional Resilience	Supports Overall Well-Being
Prayer	✓	✓	✓	✓
Contemplation	✓	✓	✓	✓
Rituals	✓	✓	✓	✓
Awe Experiences	✓	✓	✓	✓

Practice	Reduces Stress	Improves Focus	Enhances Emotional Resilience	Supports Overall Well-Being
Balanced Meals	✓	✓	✓	
Hydration		✓	✓	
Exercise	✓	✓		✓
Mindful Eating	✓		✓	✓
Daily Breaks/Rest	✓			✓

The next chapter will highlight scientific research that provides a strong foundation for Somatic Healing. It will include some information you already have learned as a review, and then will go into more depth on the topic.

Chapter 9

SCIENTIFIC BACKING AND RESEARCH

The body is a self-healing organism, so it's really about clearing things out of the way so the body can heal itself.

-- BARBARA BRENNAN

HAVE YOU EVER WONDERED or asked the question, "Is it possible to change how we think and feel by focusing on our bodies?" For many decades, the idea that our brains could reorganize and form new neural connections seemed almost magical. Now that we know it is true, the concept will give you hope and a new perspective on healing.

This chapter will explore the fascinating science of neuroplasticity and its relevance to bodily therapy. If you are interested in diving deeper into the scientific studies behind Somatic Therapy, the Resource section has many links to websites and educational papers. The overview in this chapter is a birds-eye view rather than delving too deeply into the scientific jargon.

The Science of Neuroplasticity in Somatic Therapy

Neuroplasticity is the brain's remarkable ability to reorganize itself by forming new neural connections throughout life. This capacity is essential for learning, memory, and recovery from brain injuries. In the context of Somatic Therapy, neuroplasticity plays a crucial role in healing from trauma and improving emotional regulation.

When we experience trauma, our brains can get "stuck" in patterns of fear and stress. However, we can encourage the brain to form new, healthier patterns through targeted practices. This adaptability is the cornerstone of how Somatic Therapy helps us heal from past wounds and build resilience.

The biological mechanisms that facilitate neuroplasticity are intricate and fascinating. Synaptic plasticity involves the strengthening and weakening of synapses, which are the connections between neurons. When we consistently engage in positive practices like Mindfulness or Body Awareness, these synapses strengthen, making it easier for our brains to maintain these beneficial states.

Another key mechanism is neurogenesis, which is the creation of new neurons. This process is particularly active in areas of the brain, like the hippocampus, which is involved in memory and emotional regulation. Brain-derived neurotrophic factor (BDNF) supports this neural growth, acting as a brain fertilizer. BDNF helps existing neurons survive and encourages the growth of new ones, facilitating the brain's ability to adapt and change.

In practical terms, Somatic Therapy utilizes neuroplasticity to achieve therapeutic outcomes. Techniques such as Mindfulness, Body Awareness, and Breathwork are designed to stimulate neuroplasticity. For example, Mindfulness practices help reduce activity in the amygdala, the brain's fear center, and increase connectivity in the prefrontal cortex, which is responsible for higher-order thinking and emotional regulation. This shift can lead to a more balanced and adaptive response to stress.

Case studies have shown that individuals who engage in regular somatic practices experience significant changes in brain function. Neuroimaging studies, like those using functional MRI (fMRI), reveal increased activation in brain areas associated with emotional regulation and decreased activation in areas linked to stress and anxiety.

Scientific evidence supporting the role of neuroplasticity in Somatic Therapy is growing. Research studies on trauma recovery have demonstrated the positive impact of neuroplasticity-focused interventions.

One study found that Mindfulness meditation increased gray matter density in the hippocampus, which is crucial for emotional regulation and memory. Another study using positron emission tomography (PET) scans showed that participants who practiced somatic techniques had reduced activity in the default mode network (DMN), a brain network associated with rumination and self-referential thinking. These findings suggest that Somatic Therapy not only helps manage trauma but also promotes overall mental well-being by rewiring the brain.

By consistently engaging in Mindfulness, Body Awareness, and Breathwork, you can harness the power of neuroplasticity to heal and thrive. Whether you're dealing with past trauma or simply looking to improve your emotional health, these practices offer a tangible way to create positive changes in your brain and life. The science behind neuroplasticity is not just theoretical, it's a practical, powerful tool for transformation.

Polyvagal Theory: Understanding the Nervous System

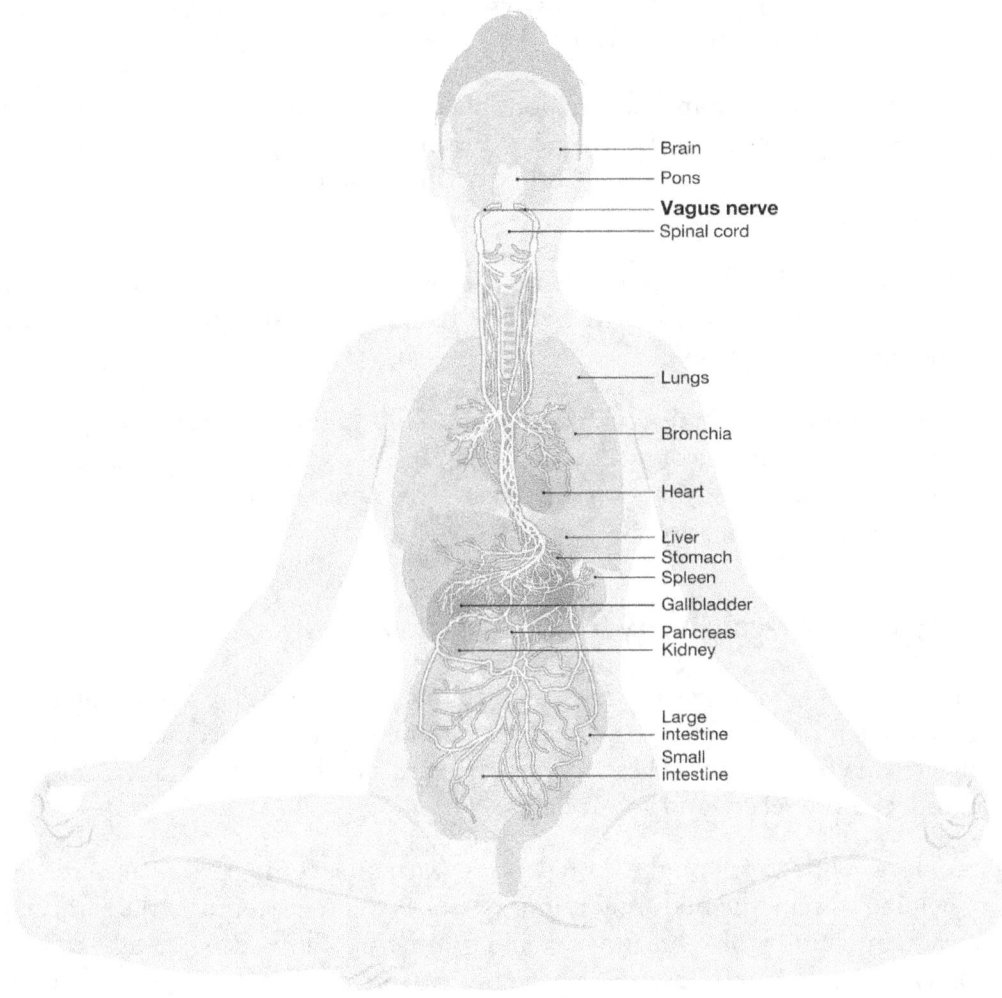

This picture shows all the internal organs that are affected by the vagus nerve.

Polyvagal Theory has been a game-changer in understanding how our nervous system impacts our emotional and physical well-being. Developed by Dr. Stephen Porges, this theory sheds light on the vagus nerve's role in regulating our physiological states.

The vagus nerve, which runs from the brainstem to the abdomen, plays a crucial role in managing our stress responses. It helps control heart rate, digestion, and even facial expressions. Porges' contributions to this field have revealed that the vagus nerve is not just about fight-or-flight responses but is also key to our social engagement system. This system allows us to feel safe and connected to others, which is vital for healing and emotional regulation.

Three Components of Polyvagal Theory

Polyvagal Theory breaks down the vagal system into three main components: the ventral vagal complex, the sympathetic nervous system, and the dorsal vagal complex. Each element has a distinct role in how we respond to stress and trauma.

- The ventral vagal complex is responsible for social engagement and connection. When this system is active, we feel safe and can engage positively with others. It's why making eye contact, smiling, or hearing a soothing voice can make us feel more at ease.

- On the other hand, the sympathetic nervous system is our body's fight-or-flight response. It kicks in when we perceive danger, preparing us to either confront the threat or run away.

- The dorsal vagal complex is linked to immobilization and shutdown. This system can cause us to freeze or feel numb in the face of overwhelming stress or trauma. Understanding these components helps us see why we might react differently in various stressful situations.

How to Apply Polyvagal Theory to Somatic Therapy

In Somatic Therapy, Polyvagal Theory is applied in several practical ways to help regulate the nervous system. Techniques to activate the ventral vagal complex include safe touch, eye contact, and vocalizations. These actions can stimulate the social engagement system, making us feel more secure and connected.

For example, a gentle touch on the shoulder or a warm, reassuring voice can activate this system, helping to calm the body and mind. Exercises to down-regulate the sympathetic nervous system often involve breathwork and grounding. Slow, deep breaths can signal to the body that it's safe to relax, while grounding exercises like feeling your feet on the floor can anchor you in the present moment, reducing anxiety.

Strategies to avoid dorsal vagal shutdown focus on gradual exposure and Titration. By slowly and safely introducing stressful stimuli, we can prevent the body from becoming overwhelmed and shutting down.

Research supports the application of Polyvagal Theory in Somatic Therapy. Studies have shown that improving vagal tone, which is the activity of the vagus nerve, can enhance emotional regulation. A higher vagal tone is associated with better stress management and inner strength.

One study found that individuals who practiced Polyvagal-informed interventions, such as Breathwork and Grounding, had reduced symptoms of anxiety and depression. Neuroimaging studies have further validated these findings. For instance, functional MRI scans have shown increased activation in brain areas responsible for emotional regulation following Polyvagal-informed therapy. These findings highlight the effectiveness of somatic techniques in promoting mental health and well-being.

Case studies also demonstrate the practical benefits of applying Polyvagal principles in therapy. One client, who had struggled with chronic anxiety, found significant relief through Polyvagal-informed Breathwork and Grounding exercises. By regularly practicing these techniques, they were able to reduce their anxiety levels and improve their overall quality of life.

Another client, who had experienced trauma, benefited from safe touch and eye contact exercises. These practices helped them feel more connected and less isolated, facilitating emotional healing. These real-life examples underscore the transformative potential of Polyvagal Theory when integrated into Somatic Therapy.

Understanding the nervous system's role in trauma and healing through the lens of Polyvagal Theory offers valuable insights and practical tools. We can foster a sense of safety and connection by activating the ventral vagal complex, downregulating the sympathetic nervous system, and avoiding dorsal vagal shutdown. This approach not only aids in managing stress and trauma but also enhances our ability to connect with others and navigate life's challenges with greater ease.

Research Studies Supporting Somatic Techniques

When I first started exploring Somatic Therapy, I wanted to know if solid evidence was behind it. I needed to see that the techniques I was learning had been studied and proven effective. This search for validation led me to a wealth of research supporting the power of somatic approaches. Evidence-based practice is crucial in therapy because it ensures that our methods are backed by scientific research. This gives therapists and clients confidence that the techniques are effective and safe. Many of those resources are listed for you in the Resource Section.

Levine's Somatic Experiencing Therapy

One of the most compelling studies in Somatic Therapy was conducted by Peter Levine, the founder of Somatic Experiencing (SE). You may already recall that Levine's research focused on how the body holds onto trauma and how physical interventions can help release it. Techniques in SE involve tracking bodily sensations, Grounding exercises, and Titration—which gradually introduce trauma-related stimuli in a controlled manner. His studies showed that somatic techniques could significantly reduce symptoms of PTSD and other trauma-related conditions.

By focusing on the body's sensations and movements, Levine found that clients could process and release trauma without needing to relive the traumatic event in detail. This approach has been groundbreaking in trauma therapy, offering a gentler yet effective way to heal. This will be discussed more thoroughly in Chapter 11.

Another critical area of research involves the impact of body awareness and mindfulness on trauma recovery. Studies have shown that Body Scanning and Mindful Movement can improve emotional regulation and reduce stress.

For example, a study published in the Journal of Traumatic Stress found that mindfulness-based interventions, which include Body Awareness exercises, significantly reduced PTSD symptoms in veterans. These findings highlight the importance of integrating body-focused practices into trauma therapy, as they address the physical manifestations of trauma that traditional talk therapy might miss.

Breathwork and Grounding exercises have also been extensively studied, with research demonstrating their benefits for mental health. A study published in *Frontiers in Psychology* found that Breathwork techniques, such as Diaphragmatic and Alternate Nostril Breathing, improved emotional regulation and reduced anxiety levels in participants. Grounding exercises, which involve connecting with the present moment through physical sensations, have been shown to reduce anxiety and panic attacks. These studies prove that Somatic Techniques can effectively manage stress and improve physical, mental, and spiritual well-being.

In research, it's essential to understand the differences between quantitative and qualitative studies. Quantitative research involves statistical analyses and measurable outcomes, providing concrete data on the effectiveness of somatic techniques. For instance, a quantitative study might measure changes in PTSD symptoms before and after Somatic Therapy using standardized questionnaires. These studies offer clear, objective evidence of the benefits of somatic practices.

On the other hand, qualitative research focuses on personal narratives and case studies, offering a more nuanced understanding of how Somatic Techniques impact individuals. Qualitative studies involve in-depth interviews with clients undergoing Somatic Therapy, exploring their experiences and the changes they've noticed. Both types of research are valuable, as they provide complementary insights. Quantitative studies offer broad, generalizable data, while qualitative studies provide rich, detailed accounts of individual experiences.

The practical implications of these research findings are significant for therapists and clients. Therapists can confidently integrate these evidence-based techniques into their practice, knowing they are supported by scientific research. This can enhance the effectiveness of their therapy sessions and provide clients with a more comprehensive approach to healing. For clients, knowing that the techniques they are using have been rigorously studied can increase their confidence and commitment to the therapy process.

Ongoing research is vital in advancing the field of Somatic Therapy. As new studies emerge, they continue to refine our understanding of how these techniques work and how they can be improved. This constant evolution ensures that Somatic Therapy remains at the cutting edge of trauma and stress treatment, offering hope and healing to those in need. In the next section, we'll explore evidence-based practices for trauma healing, diving deeper into the specific techniques validated by research.

Evidence-Based Practices for Trauma Healing

When discussing evidence-based practices in trauma healing, we refer to methods rigorously tested and proven effective through scientific research. These practices are not just theoretical; they have demonstrated efficacy, safety, and replicability.

Using evidence-based practices means therapists can trust their methods, knowing they are supported by solid research. For clients, it provides confidence that the techniques they are engaging with have a track record of success, making the healing process more reliable and trustworthy. This dual assurance is crucial for building a therapeutic alliance and fostering a sense of security in the healing journey.

- Sensorimotor Psychotherapy (SP) is another evidence-based somatic practice that integrates Body Awareness and Movement with cognitive and emotional processing. SP helps individuals process trauma by focusing on the physical sensations and movements associated with traumatic memories. Research has shown that SP can improve emotional regulation and reduce trauma symptoms. A study in the *European Journal of Psychotraumatology* found that SP significantly decreased PTSD symptoms and improved emotional functioning in survivors of childhood abuse. By addressing the somatic aspects of trauma, SP provides a comprehensive approach to healing.

- Trauma-informed yoga is also gaining recognition as an effective somatic practice for trauma healing. This approach adapts traditional yoga practices to be sensitive to the needs of trauma survivors. Techniques include Mindful Movement, Breathwork, and Body Awareness exercises designed to create a sense of safety and empowerment. Scientific validation of Trauma-Informed Yoga comes from studies showing its benefits in reducing PTSD symptoms and improving emotional well-being. Research published in the *Journal of Clinical Psychology* found that participants in a Trauma-Informed Yoga program experienced significant reductions in PTSD symptoms and improvements in overall mental health.

- Cognitive-behavioral therapy (CBT) can provide a holistic approach to trauma healing. CBT addresses the cognitive aspects of trauma, while somatic practices focus on the physical sensations and movements. This integration allows for a more comprehensive treatment addressing mind and body.

- Eye Movement Desensitization and Reprocessing (EMDR) can enhance the processing of traumatic memories. EMDR as part of Somatic Therapy focuses on desensitizing and reprocessing traumatic memories, while somatic practices help release the physical tension associated with those memories. Pendulation is often used as part of the EMDR exercise. EMDR therapists often use pendulation, a somatic practice, to help clients shift between distressing memories and feelings of safety. For instance, if a memory triggers overwhelming body sensations, the therapist might guide the client to focus on a "resource" (a positive or neutral sensation in the body) before returning to the trauma. This is best used with a therapist, not on your own.

This process mirrors the body's natural rhythm of moving between activation and relaxation.

Complementing pharmacotherapy (the use of medications) with Somatic Techniques can also provide a balanced approach to trauma healing. This is another time when it's best to work with a therapist, not on your own.

Reducing Long-Term Dependence on Medications

Somatic therapy equips individuals with body-based tools to self-regulate and process difficult emotions, potentially decreasing their reliance on medications over time. This is particularly beneficial for those concerned about dependency or side effects of long-term pharmacotherapy.

For instance, someone using medication to manage panic attacks might gradually shift to relying on somatic techniques like grounding, breathwork, or body scanning to achieve similar results.

While medication can help manage symptoms, somatic practices address the underlying physiological and emotional aspects of trauma, providing a more holistic treatment. The goal would be to use medication to manage symptoms while learning to use Somatic Therapy as an alternative to gradually decrease the need for the medication.

Summary

The future of research in Somatic Therapy and trauma healing is promising. Emerging areas of interest include Virtual Reality and Biofeedback in Somatic Therapy. Virtual reality can create immersive environments that help individuals safely confront and process traumatic memories. At the same time, Biofeedback provides real-time data on physiological responses, assisting individuals in learning to regulate their stress responses.

Longitudinal studies are crucial for understanding the long-term outcomes of Somatic Therapy. These studies can track the progress of individuals over extended periods, providing valuable insights into the lasting effects of somatic practices.

Collaboration between researchers, therapists, and clients is essential for continued innovation in the field. By working together, we can develop new techniques, refine existing practices, and ensure that Somatic Therapy continues to evolve and improve.

Here are the summary charts for the somatic exercises in this chapter.

Technique	Ease of Practice	Time Commitment
Mindfulness Practices	Easy	5–10 mins
Breathwork	Easy	5 mins
Body Awareness	Moderate	5–10 mins
Safe Touch	Easy	5 mins
Grounding	Easy	5 mins
Eye Contact	Easy	5–10 mins
Somatic Experiencing (SE)	Moderate	Varies
Sensorimotor Psychotherapy (SP)	Moderate	Varies
Trauma-Informed Yoga	Moderate	30 mins
EMDR with Pendulation	Challenging	30 mins
Somatic Therapy with Medications	Easy	Varies
Grounding and Breathwork (Self-Regulation)	Easy	10–20 mins

Technique	Improves Emotional Regulation	Reduces Stress	Improves Memory	Facilitates Trauma Recovery
Mindfulness Practices	✓	✓	✓	✓
Breathwork	✓	✓		✓
Body Awareness	✓	✓		✓

Technique	Regulates Nervous System	Enhances Emotional Stability	Improves Connection
Breathwork	✓	✓	✓
Safe Touch	✓	✓	✓
Grounding	✓	✓	✓
Eye Contact	✓	✓	✓

Technique	Reduces PTSD Symptoms	Improves Emotional Regulation	Supports Holistic Healing
Somatic Experiencing (SE)	✓	✓	✓
Sensorimotor Psychotherapy (SP)	✓	✓	✓
Trauma-Informed Yoga	✓	✓	✓
EMDR with Pendulation	✓	✓	✓

Technique	Reduces PTSD Symptoms	Improves Emotional Regulation	Supports Holistic Healing
Somatic Therapy with Medications	✓	✓	✓
Grounding and Breathwork (Self-Regulation)	✓	✓	✓

In the next chapter, we will explore how to build a supportive community around your healing process, emphasizing the importance of connection and shared experiences in your journey.

Chapter 10

BUILDING A SUPPORTIVE COMMUNITY

Your body is not a reflection of your worth.
It's a vessel for your journey.

-- UNKNOWN

HAVING A SUPPORTIVE COMMUNITY around you is critical in your healing journey. This chapter explores how building a healing network can be a cornerstone of your recovery journey.

Creating a Healing Network

Having a supportive network is crucial for the healing process. It provides emotional support and understanding, which can make all the difference when navigating difficult times. When you feel understood and supported, you feel less isolated and lonely. A supportive network acts as a safety net, offering comfort and reassurance that you are not alone in your struggles.

Additionally, a supportive community encourages accountability and consistency in your healing practices. Knowing that others are cheering you on and holding you accountable can motivate you to stick with your routines, even on tough days. Furthermore, a diverse network offers various perspectives and shared experiences, enriching your journey with different insights and wisdom.

Identifying potential members for your healing network is the next step to creating this type of community. Start by looking at your circle of friends and family members. Who among them is empathetic and supportive? These individuals can be invaluable allies in your healing process. Consider colleagues or acquaintances who share your interest in holistic health. They might be interested in joining you for activities like yoga or meditation, providing mutual support. Professionals and therapists can also be a part of your network, offering expert advice and guidance. Their experience and knowledge can be beneficial in navigating complex emotional landscapes.

Building and maintaining these connections requires effort and intention. Regular check-ins and meetings help keep the lines of communication open. Creating a communication plan can also be helpful. Group chats or video calls can keep everyone connected and informed. Setting mutual goals and supporting each other's progress fosters a sense of shared purpose and commitment. When everyone is working towards similar objectives, it strengthens the bond within the group.

Equally important is creating a safe and nonjudgmental space where members feel comfortable sharing. Establishing ground rules for respectful communication is essential. Encourage open and honest discussions where everyone feels heard and valued. Addressing conflicts constructively and maintaining trust is crucial for the longevity and health of the network. When conflicts arise, handle them with empathy and a focus on resolution, ensuring that the space remains supportive and inclusive.

Reflection Exercise: Building Your Healing Network

1. **Identify Key Individuals:** List friends, family members, colleagues, and professionals you believe can be part of your healing network. Reflect on the qualities that make them supportive and empathetic.

2. **Initiate Conversations:** Reach out to these individuals and share your healing goals. Discuss how you would like them to be part of your journey and how you can support each other.

3. **Set Up Regular Check-Ins:** Plan regular meetings or check-ins. Consistency is key, whether weekly phone calls, monthly gatherings, or online chats.

4. **Create Ground Rules:** Establish ground rules for communication within your network. Ensure everyone understands the importance of respect, empathy, and confidentiality.

5. **Reflect and Adjust:** Periodically reflect on the dynamics of your network. Are the connections supportive and helpful? Are there areas that need adjustment? Make changes as necessary to maintain a healthy and supportive network.

By taking these steps, you can build a robust healing network that provides emotional support, encourages accountability, and offers diverse perspectives. This network will be your anchor, helping you navigate the ups and downs of your healing journey.

Online Forums and Support Groups

Online support groups and forums can offer a lifeline when you feel isolated or overwhelmed. One of the most significant advantages of joining online communities is accessibility and convenience. You can connect with others from the comfort of your home at any time of day. This flexibility means you can find support whenever needed without worrying about scheduling conflicts or travel.

Online platforms unite people worldwide, offering diverse perspectives and shared experiences that can enrich your understanding and provide new insights. Additionally, online forums offer the option of anonymity, which can be especially comforting for those who may feel hesitant to share their struggles openly.

Finding reputable online communities is crucial for ensuring a positive and supportive experience. Start by checking if the forum or support group is professionally moderated. Professional moderation helps maintain a respectful and constructive environment. Reading reviews and testimonials from other users can give you a sense of the community's culture and effectiveness.

Assess the quality of discussions and resources provided—are the conversations meaningful and supportive? Do the resources offered seem credible and valuable? Popular forums like Reddit's r/somatic therapy can be excellent starting points, but always take the time to evaluate each community carefully. If you are a Facebook user, several Somatic Therapy groups are available for ongoing support.

Once you've found a reputable online community, actively participating can significantly enhance your experience. Introduce yourself and share your story. This initial step can feel daunting, but it's a powerful way to connect with others and start building relationships.

Don't hesitate to ask questions and seek advice. Most community members are eager to help and share their experiences. Offering support and encouragement to others helps them and fosters a sense of belonging and reciprocity. Participating in group challenges and activities can also be a fun and engaging way to stay involved and motivated.

While online support can be incredibly beneficial, it is essential to balance it with offline interactions. Combining online resources with in-person meetings can provide a more rounded support system. Without the in-person meetings, you may feel isolated.

For instance, you might participate in an online forum during the week and attend a local support group on weekends. Using online support as a supplement rather than a replacement ensures you maintain real-world connections, which are equally important for emotional well-being. Setting boundaries is crucial to prevent over-reliance on online communities. Set limits on your time online and engage in other activities that bring you joy and fulfillment.

Online support groups and forums offer a unique and valuable way to connect with others who understand your experiences. Whether you need advice, want to share your progress, or need a listening ear, online communities can provide the support and encouragement you need.

Finding Qualified Somatic Therapists

Having professional guidance is crucial for effective healing. A qualified Somatic Therapist brings expertise in Somatic Techniques, which is essential for navigating the complexities of trauma and stress stored in the body. They provide personalized guidance and support tailored to your unique needs and experiences. This one-on-one attention ensures that the techniques are applied correctly and effectively.

Furthermore, professional therapists have access to advanced therapeutic practices that can significantly enhance the healing process. They continuously update their skills and knowledge through ongoing education and training, ensuring you benefit from the latest advancements in bodily therapy.

Selecting the right therapist involves careful consideration of several criteria. First, look for professional certifications and training. A therapist who has completed a recognized certification program in Somatic Therapy demonstrates a commitment to their field and a thorough understanding of the techniques.

Next, consider their experience and specialization. Therapists with extensive experience in Somatic Treatment are more likely to have encountered a wide range of issues and developed effective strategies for addressing them. Specialization in areas such as trauma recovery or chronic pain can be particularly beneficial if you have specific needs. Positive reviews and client testimonials can also provide valuable insights into a therapist's effectiveness and approach. Reading about others' experiences can help you gauge whether a therapist's style and methods resonate with you.

Finding qualified Somatic Therapists can seem daunting, but several practical ways exist to begin your search. Online directories of certified Somatic Therapists are a great resource. Websites like the Somatic Experiencing Trauma Institute and Psychology Today's therapist directory allow you to search for professionals based on location, specialization, and certifications.

Referrals from healthcare providers or support groups can also lead you to reputable therapists. These referrals often come with personal recommendations and insights into the therapist's approach and effectiveness. Professional associations dedicated to Somatic Therapy can also be valuable resources. They usually maintain directories of certified practitioners and provide information on ongoing education and training.

Schedule an Initial Consultation

The initial consultation with a potential therapist is a critical step in the selection process. This meeting allows you to assess whether the therapist fits you well. Prepare a list of questions about their approach and experience. Ask about their training, how they integrate somatic techniques into their practice, and their experience with issues similar to yours.

Assess the therapist's communication style and empathy during this interaction. Notice how they respond to your questions and concerns. Do they listen attentively? Do they make you feel heard and understood? Discussing your goals and expectations for therapy is also essential. Clearly articulate what you hope to achieve and listen to how the therapist plans to help you reach those goals. This conversation can determine whether their approach aligns with your needs.

Comfort and trust are the foundation of any therapeutic relationship. Pay attention to how you feel during the consultation. Do you feel comfortable and at ease? Can you imagine building a trusting relationship with this therapist? Trust your instincts. If something doesn't feel right, continuing your search is okay. The right therapist will have the qualifications and experience to make you feel safe and supported. This sense of safety is crucial for the vulnerable work of Somatic Therapy.

Finding a qualified Somatic Therapist may take time and effort, but it is an investment in your healing and well-being. The right professional can provide the expertise, guidance, and support you need to navigate your healing journey effectively. As you embark on this search, remember that the goal is to find someone who has the right qualifications and feels like a good fit for you personally.

Encouragement and Support in Your Healing Journey

Encouragement plays a vital role in the healing process. It boosts motivation and perseverance, especially when you feel like giving up. When someone believes in you, it instills a sense of hope and determination. This external validation can make it easier to keep going, even when the path ahead seems daunting.

Encouragement also helps reduce feelings of isolation and loneliness. Knowing that others are cheering you on can make a significant difference, transforming solitary struggles into shared journeys. This support enhances self-confidence and resilience, making you feel more capable of facing challenges.

Various sources of encouragement can provide the support you need. Family and friends who understand and support your healing efforts are invaluable. They offer security and unconditional love, making opening up and sharing your experiences easier. Peer support from others undergoing similar experiences can be remarkably empowering. Connecting with people who truly understand your struggles can provide unique insights and mutual encouragement.

Inspirational stories and testimonials from those who have successfully navigated their healing journeys can also be a powerful source of motivation. These stories remind you that healing is possible and provide practical examples of how others have overcome similar challenges.

Self-Encouragement Ideas

Practicing self-encouragement is equally important. Daily affirmations and positive self-talk help maintain a positive mindset. Start your day with affirmations like, "I am strong and capable," or "I am making progress daily." These statements can set a positive tone and reinforce your self-belief.

Celebrating small victories and progress is another effective way to encourage yourself. Acknowledge your achievements, no matter how minor they may seem. Each step forward is a testament to your strength and determination. Reflecting on personal strengths and achievements can also boost your self-confidence. Recognize the qualities and skills that have helped you navigate difficult times. This reflection can provide a sense of pride and motivate you to continue your efforts.

Building a long-term support system requires ongoing effort and commitment. Establishing ongoing support groups or accountability partners can provide consistent encouragement and motivation. These groups offer a structured way to share experiences, set goals, and celebrate achievements. Regularly updating and seeking new resources and connections can enhance your support system. Stay open to new opportunities and relationships that can offer additional support and insights.

Continually nurturing and investing in supportive relationships is crucial for maintaining a solid support system. Make an effort to show appreciation and provide support to others in your network. This reciprocity strengthens the bonds within the group and ensures that everyone feels valued and supported.

Summary

In conclusion, encouragement and support are essential components of the healing journey. This support can significantly impact your motivation, confidence, and resilience, whether from family, friends, peers, or self-encouragement practices. By building and maintaining a solid support system, you create a foundation to help you navigate the challenges and celebrate the victories.

In the next chapter, you'll find advanced techniques for Somatic Therapy and explore what it's like to feel fully present in your body. Again, we'll start with the basics that you already know and understand, and then build upon them to give you more depth to the topic.

Chapter 11

ADVANCED TECHNIQUES IN SOMATIC THERAPY

The body is like a piano, and happiness is like music.
It's needful to have the instrument in good order.

-- HENRY WARD BEECHER

Embodiment: Being Fully Present in Your Body

EMBODIMENT IS THE PRACTICE of being fully present in one's body. It involves a deep connection with bodily sensations, allowing you to experience and process emotions more effectively.

Have you ever noticed a small child playing with their toys? They are utterly absorbed in the moment. You realize that the child is fully embodied, present in their body and the moment. Embodiment, in Somatic Therapy, is about reclaiming that kind of presence. It means being fully attuned to your physical sensations, emotions, and thoughts without judgment. Instead of living in our heads, we engage with our bodies, experiencing life more vividly and authentically.

Unlike intellectual understanding, which often stays in the realm of thoughts, embodiment brings awareness to the physical realm. This practice has profound benefits for both emotional and physical health. Emotionally, it helps you process feelings by noticing where they manifest in the body. Physically, it can reduce tension and stress.

For instance, understanding stress on an intellectual level might help you realize you're overworked, but feeling it as a tightness in your shoulders prompts you to relax immediately.

How to Get Better at Embodiment

To enhance embodiment, start with Body Meditations. These Guided Meditations focus on bodily sensations, helping you become aware of how your body feels in the present moment. You might sit quietly and scan your body from head to toe, noticing areas of tension or comfort. This practice increases your body awareness and helps you release stored tension.

Dynamic Movement Practices

Another powerful technique is Dynamic Movement practices, such as dance or yoga. These activities encourage you to move your body in natural and expressive ways, promoting a deeper connection with your physical self. Sensory Immersion is another technique that involves engaging all your senses to deepen your connection with your body. This could mean paying close attention to the sounds, smells, and textures around you.

For example, you might practice Body Scans while engaging in slow, deliberate movements, noticing how each movement feels in your muscles and joints.

Mindful Walking

Using embodiment practices in your daily routine can be transformative. Mindful Walking is a simple yet effective practice. As you walk, focus on the sensation of each step. Notice how your feet feel as they contact the ground and pay attention to the rhythm of your stride. This practice grounds you in the present moment and enhances your connection with your body.

Eating with Awareness

Another practice is Eating with Awareness. Instead of rushing through meals, take the time to savor each bite. Pay attention to the taste, texture, and smell of your food. This enhances your eating experience and helps you tune into your body's hunger and fullness cues.

Embodied Listening

Embodied Listening is another powerful practice. When listening to someone, fully engage with your bodily sensations. Notice how their words make you feel physically. This practice improves your listening skills and helps you stay present in conversations.

Challenges of Embodiment

Practicing embodiment can be challenging, but there are solutions. One common challenge is overcoming distractions. In our fast-paced world, it's easy for your mind to wander. To enhance focus, try setting specific times for your embodiment practices and creating a peaceful environment. Listening to calming music or nature sounds can also help.

Another challenge is dealing with discomfort. When you start paying attention to your body, you might notice areas of tension or pain. Instead of avoiding these sensations, try to stay present with them. Breathe into the discomfort and observe it without judgment. You'll often find that the sensation lessens over time.

Balancing embodiment with daily responsibilities can also take time and effort. It's essential to integrate these practices into your routine without feeling overwhelmed. Start small, perhaps with a few minutes of Mindful Walking or a short Body Scan. As you become more comfortable, you can increase your time on these practices.

Embodiment is about reclaiming your relationship with your body. It's about feeling alive and present, not just going through the motions of life. Integrating these practices into your routine can enhance your emotional and physical well-being. Whether through body meditation, Mindful Walking, or simply paying attention to your senses, each step brings you closer to being fully present in your body. So, remember the child playing with their toys next time you feel stressed or disconnected. Let yourself be fully present and embrace the joy of being alive in your body.

Somatic Experiencing: Advanced Trauma Healing

Somatic Experiencing (SE) was mentioned earlier in this book but now we'll take the topic in more detail. SE is a profound approach to trauma healing that goes beyond basic somatic practices. Developed by Dr. Peter Levine, SE is grounded in the idea that trauma is not just a psychological issue but a physical one as well. Trauma gets stored in the body, creating a state of constant dysregulation in the nervous system. SE aims to release this stored trauma through bodily interventions, helping the nervous system return to normal functionality.

Since SE focuses on bodily sensations and uses them as a gateway to explore and resolve trauma, this method is particularly beneficial for deep trauma healing. It addresses the root of the issue rather than just the symptoms. Levine's contributions have been instrumental in shaping SE, emphasizing the importance of completing the "incomplete biological response to a threat" that trauma creates.

Tracking and Titration

One of the core techniques in Somatic Experiencing is Tracking and Titration. This involves closely monitoring bodily sensations and gradually exposing oneself to traumatic memories in a controlled manner. The idea is to approach these memories slowly, allowing the nervous system to process them without becoming overwhelmed. By doing this, you can release stored tension and reduce the impact of trauma on your daily life.

Resourcing

Another critical technique is Resourcing, which involves building internal and external "lists" of positive experiences to be used as resources to draw upon for the purpose of creating a sense of safety. This could involve imagining a safe place or relying on supportive relationships.

Pendulation and Discharge

Pendulation and Discharge are also crucial in SE. Pendulation involves moving between states of arousal and relaxation, helping you release trauma in manageable doses. Discharge, on the other hand, is about releasing the energy that gets trapped in the body due to trauma. Techniques like Shaking or Deep Breathing can facilitate this release, making it easier to process deep-seated trauma.

Finding Proof From Testimonials

Case studies and success stories provide compelling evidence of the effectiveness of Somatic Experiencing. Take, for example, a veteran recovering from PTSD. After years of struggling with flashbacks and anxiety, he found relief through SE. Focusing on bodily sensations and using techniques like Tracking and Titration, he was able to process traumatic memories without becoming overwhelmed. Over time, his symptoms reduced, allowing him to feel more peaceful.

Another powerful example is a survivor of childhood abuse who found healing through SE. She had tried various therapies with little success until she discovered SE. The practice of Resourcing helped her create a sense of safety, while Pendulation allowed her to release stored trauma gradually. Testimonials from clients who have experienced significant trauma release through SE further highlight its transformative power. They often speak of newfound freedom and emotional stability they hadn't achieved with other therapies.

Combining Somatic Experiencing with Other Techniques

Integrating Somatic Experiencing with other therapeutic approaches can offer a holistic healing experience. Combining SE with Cognitive-Behavioral Therapy (CBT) can be particularly effective. While SE addresses the physical symptoms of trauma, CBT focuses on reshaping dysfunctional thoughts. Together, they provide a comprehensive approach to trauma healing.

Mindfulness and Meditation practices also complement SE, enhancing body awareness and emotional regulation. Techniques like Mindful Breathing and Body Scans can help you stay present and grounded, making it easier to engage with SE practices.

Eye Movement Desensitization and Reprocessing (EMDR) is another therapy that works well alongside SE. EMDR uses bilateral stimulation to process traumatic memories, while SE focuses on bodily sensations. By integrating these methods, you can address both the cognitive and physical aspects of trauma, leading to more effective and lasting healing.

Advanced Breathwork Techniques

In Somatic Therapy, advanced breathwork techniques hold a unique place. Breath is not just a means of oxygenating the body but a powerful tool in regulating the nervous system. By consciously controlling your breath, you can influence your emotional state and release deep-seated trauma. Basic breathwork practices, like Diaphragmatic and Box Breathing, are excellent for everyday stress management.

However, advanced techniques take this practice to the next level, offering profound benefits for emotional release and trauma healing. Below are three advanced methods that engage your body and mind more intensely, facilitating deeper emotional and physical healing. Because of the nature of these advanced methods, it is recommended that you use them with the guidance of a certified practitioner.

- Holotropic Breathwork, for instance, is an advanced technique designed for deep emotional release. Developed by psychiatrist Stanislav Grof, this method involves rapid, rhythmic breathing patterns combined with evocative music to induce an altered state of consciousness. Acknowledging, accessing, and supporting each individual's inner healing intelligence and impulse is the essential cornerstone of this approach. This state allows you to access and process repressed emotions and trauma. <u>Practicing Holotropic breathwork involves several steps. Here's the procedure:</u>

  a. Find a comfortable, safe environment where you won't be disturbed. Lie down and close your eyes.

  b. Start with deep, rhythmic breaths.

  c. Gradually increase the speed and intensity of your breathing, maintaining a continuous, rhythmic pattern. As you breathe, allow the evocative music to guide you, letting any emotions or sensations arise without judgment. This intense breathing can lead to powerful emotional releases, so it's crucial to have a supportive environment.

d. After the session, take time to rest and reflect on your experience, perhaps journaling your thoughts and feelings.

- Transformational Breathwork is another powerful method that uses specific breath patterns to release trauma. Focusing on continuous, connected breaths allows you to bypass the conscious mind and tap into the body's stored emotional energy.

- Rebirthing Breathwork, as the name suggests, focuses on birth-related trauma. This technique uses circular breathing to revisit and heal traumatic birth experiences, often leading to profound emotional release. These advanced techniques go beyond simple relaxation, targeting deeper layers of emotional and physical tension.

This practice can be intense, so it's essential to approach it with care and respect for your body's limits.

Safety During Advanced Breathwork

Safety is paramount when practicing advanced breathwork techniques. You might think that since everyone breathes, then doing breathwork is a no-brainer. However, breathwork can have powerful effects on the body and mind. If they aren't done properly, they could lead to negative effects.

Here are some guidelines to help you stay safe:

1. Always ensure you're in a safe, comfortable environment where you can fully relax.

2. Be aware of any contraindications. Individuals with cardiovascular issues, high blood pressure, or a history of seizures should avoid intense breathwork practices.

3. If you're pregnant or have severe mental health conditions, consult a healthcare provider before beginning.

4. Preparing mentally and physically for these sessions is also essential. Set a clear intention for your practice and ensure you're in a calm, focused state of mind.

5. Hydrate well and avoid heavy meals before your session.

Being mindful of these guidelines ensures a safe and effective practice.

In therapeutic settings, Advanced Breathwork can be a powerful preparatory tool. Using Breathwork at the beginning of a session can help clients enter a more relaxed, open state, making them more receptive to deeper somatic work.

Breathwork Plus Body Awareness Together

Combining Breathwork with Body Awareness exercises can further enhance its effectiveness. For instance, you might start with a few minutes of Holotropic breathwork to release surface tension, followed by a Body Scan to identify and address deeper areas of stored trauma. Breathwork can also serve as a closing practice in therapy sessions. After exploring intense emotions, Guided Breathwork can help integrate experiences and bring a sense of closure and calm.

These more advanced therapies offer a unique pathway to healing, allowing you to access and release emotions that might be too deep for words. If approached with care and respect, these practices can be a cornerstone of your Somatic Therapy journey.

Integrating Somatic Practices into Therapy Sessions

Integrating somatic practices into traditional therapy sessions can significantly enhance therapeutic outcomes. These practices bring a depth and holistic healing that purely cognitive approaches often miss.

Using Somatic Techniques makes the therapeutic process more effective and rewarding for clients and therapists. Somatic practices complement talk therapy by addressing the physical manifestations of emotional issues.

For example, while discussing a traumatic experience, a client might notice tightness in their chest. Through Somatic Techniques, the therapist can guide the client to focus on this sensation, helping to release stored tension and emotions. This dual approach of cognitive and somatic interventions can lead to more comprehensive healing.

Several techniques can be effectively integrated into therapy sessions to enhance the overall experience. One such technique is the Body Awareness check-in. Start each session focusing on bodily sensations to help clients tune into their physical state. This practice sets a grounded tone for the session, making clients more present and receptive.

Somatic interventions like Grounding exercises and Breathwork can be invaluable during emotional processing. These techniques help clients manage intense emotions by anchoring them in the present moment and calming their nervous system. Movement in therapy sessions is another powerful tool. Simple Stretching, Gentle Shaking, or Mindful Walking exercises can help release tension and enhance body awareness. These movements can be instrumental in assisting clients in processing and integrating emotional experiences.

Case Studies

Reading case studies illustrates the successful integration of somatic practices in therapy. One client, dealing with profound grief after the loss of a loved one, found solace in Body Awareness techniques. By focusing on the physical sensations associated with their grief, they could process their emotions more fully.

Another client, struggling with anxiety, benefited immensely from integrating Breathwork into their sessions. Techniques like Diaphragmatic Breathing and the 4-7-8 Method helped her manage her stress more effectively, both during and outside therapy sessions.

In another case, a client dealing with depression found that mixing movement into their therapy sessions made a significant difference. Simple exercises like Mindful Walking and Gentle Stretching helped him reconnect with his bodies, lifting mood and creating a more positive outlook on life.

What Therapists Need to Practice

Therapists must acquire the skills to integrate somatic practices into their sessions. Ongoing education and certification in somatic techniques ensure that therapists can offer the most effective interventions. Various training programs and workshops are available for therapists to deepen their understanding of somatic practices. Participating in these programs enhances their skills and provides professional growth and networking opportunities.

Supervision and peer support improve one's skills quickly. Regular supervision allows therapists to reflect on their practice, receive feedback, and gain new insights. Peer support groups offer a space to share experiences, discuss challenges, and learn from each other. This collaborative approach enhances the therapist's ability to integrate somatic practices effectively.

Integrating somatic practices into therapy sessions can transform the therapeutic process for both clients and therapists. Combining cognitive and somatic interventions offers a more holistic approach to healing, addressing both the mind and body.

Summary

By combining techniques such as Body Awareness check-ins, Grounding exercises, Breathwork, and Movement, therapists can create a more comprehensive and effective therapeutic experience. These practices provide clients with tools to manage emotions, release tension, and enhance well-being.

For therapists, ongoing education, supervision, and peer support ensure they can offer the most effective and up-to-date interventions. This integrated approach fosters a deeper connection between the therapist and the client, leading to more meaningful and lasting healing.

Here are the tables that summarize the somatic exercises in this chapter.

Technique	Ease of Practice	Time Commitment
Body Meditations	Easy	10–15 mins
Dynamic Movement (Dance/Yoga)	Moderate	10–20 mins
Mindful Walking	Easy	5–10 mins
Eating with Awareness	Easy	5–10 mins
Embodied Listening	Easy	5–10 mins
Tracking	Moderate	5–10 mins
Titration	Moderate	10 mins
Resourcing	Easy	5 mins
Pendulation	Moderate	10–15 mins
Discharge (Shaking/Deep Breathing)	Easy	5–10 mins
Holotropic Breathwork	Challenging	30–60 mins
Transformational Breathwork	Challenging	20–30 mins
Rebirthing Breathwork	Challenging	30–60 mins
Body Awareness Check-ins	Easy	5–10 mins
Grounding Exercises	Easy	5 mins
Movement in Sessions	Moderate	5–10 mins
Breathwork (Diaphragmatic, 4-7-8)	Easy	5–10 mins

Technique	Enhances Presence	Reduces Stress	Improves Body Awareness	Supports Emotional Regulation
Body Meditations	✓	✓	✓	✓
Dynamic Movement (Dance/Yoga)	✓	✓	✓	✓
Mindful Walking	✓	✓	✓	✓
Eating with Awareness	✓	✓	✓	✓
Embodied Listening	✓	✓	✓	✓

Technique	Releases Stored Trauma	Regulates Nervous System	Supports Emotional Stability
Tracking	✓	✓	✓
Titration	✓	✓	✓
Resourcing	✓	✓	✓
Pendulation	✓	✓	✓
Discharge (Shaking/Deep Breathing)	✓	✓	✓

Technique	Promotes Emotional Release	Facilitates Trauma Healing	Encourages Relaxation	Induces Altered Awareness
Holotropic Breathwork	✓	✓	✓	✓
Transformational Breathwork	✓	✓	✓	✓
Rebirthing Breathwork	✓	✓	✓	✓

Technique	Supports Emotional Processing	Releases Tension	Enhances Grounding	Improves Therapeutic Outcomes
Body Awareness Check-ins	✓	✓	✓	✓
Grounding Exercises	✓	✓	✓	✓
Movement in Sessions (Shaking, Stretching)	✓	✓	✓	✓
Breathwork (Diaphragmatic, 4-7-8)	✓	✓	✓	✓

Technique	Supports Emotional Processing	Releases Tension	Enhances Grounding	Improves Therapeutic Outcomes
Body Awareness Check-ins	✓	✓	✓	✓
Grounding Exercises	✓	✓	✓	✓
Movement in Sessions (Shaking, Stretching)	✓	✓	✓	✓
Breathwork (Diaphragmatic, 4-7-8)	✓	✓	✓	✓

The next chapter will explore how to create sustainable healing habits to support long-term well-being and resilience. Through practical tips and exercises, you will learn how to make these advanced somatic practices a regular part of your daily life, ensuring ongoing growth and healing.

Chapter 12

LONG-TERM HEALING AND GROWTH

The body is your temple. Keep it pure and clean for the soul to reside in.

— *B.K.S. IYENGAR*

THIS FINAL CHAPTER FOCUSES on establishing consistent and nurturing routines to create a strong foundation for a balanced and fulfilling life.

Creating Sustainable Healing Habits

The journey to long-term healing is like a marathon. Developing sustainable habits is crucial for maintaining progress and ensuring that the benefits of Somatic Therapy last. The definition of sustainable healing habits is practices that promote long-term physical, emotional, mental, and spiritual well-being. They are designed to nurture and restore balance in a way that can be consistently maintained over time. This fosters resilience and vitality without exhausting personal or environmental resources. These habits focus on prevention, self-awareness, and holistic approaches to healing.

As mentioned before, consistency is key. Regularly practicing somatic exercises and Mindfulness techniques solidify their impact. Sustainable habits help integrate these practices into daily life, making them second nature. They also provide a buffer against setbacks, ensuring that moments of struggle don't derail your progress.

Sustainable habits offer numerous benefits for mental and physical health. Regular engagement in calming practices like Breathwork or Body Scanning can reduce stress, improve sleep, and enhance comprehensive health. Sustainable routines prevent burnout by balancing active and restorative activities. Instead of exhausting yourself with constant self-improvement, you create a rhythm that rejuvenates and sustains you. This balance is essential for preventing burnout and maintaining enthusiasm for your healing journey.

Identifying the most impactful practices to incorporate into daily life is essential. Core somatic exercises like Grounding techniques, Breathwork, and Body Scans form the foundation of a healing routine. These practices reconnect you with your body and promote emotional regulation.

It's also important to prioritize activities that bring joy and relaxation. Whether it's a hobby, a walk in nature, or time spent with loved ones, these activities are vital for emotional well-being. Balancing active and restorative practices ensures that you stay engaged without feeling overwhelmed. For instance, incorporate daily Breathwork sessions and set aside time for a weekly Body Scan to check in with your physical state.

How to Create a Routine to Support Your Healing Journey

Building a routine that supports your healing journey involves setting realistic and achievable goals. Start small, and gradually increase the duration or intensity of your practices. Allocate specific times for different activities to create a structured yet flexible routine.

For example, begin your day with a short Meditation, incorporate Mindful Stretching during your lunch break, and end the day with a Body Scan before bed. Adjust your routine based on feedback and needs. If a practice feels overwhelming, scale it back or try a different approach. Listen to your body and be willing to adapt.

To maintain consistency in your healing habits, there are practical strategies to help:

1. Use reminders and planners to keep you on track and ensure that you remember to engage in your practices.

2. Seek accountability from friends or support groups. Sharing your goals and progress with others creates a sense of community and provides motivation.

3. Celebrate small victories and milestones, recognizing your achievements along the way. For example, you might track your progress in a journal or app, noting improvements in your emotional or physical well-being.

Interactive Element: Reflective Journaling Prompt

Take a moment to reflect on your current routine and identify areas where you can incorporate sustainable healing habits.

Consider the following questions in your Journal:

1. What somatic practices have been most effective for you so far?

2. How can you incorporate these practices into your daily routine?

3. What activities bring you joy and relaxation, and how can you make time for them?

4. What small, realistic goals can you set for yourself this week?

5. How will you celebrate your progress and stay motivated?

Sustainable healing habits are the building blocks of long-term well-being. By integrating core somatic exercises, prioritizing joy and relaxation, and maintaining a balanced routine, you create a foundation that supports your growth and recovery. Remember, the goal is not perfection but progress. Celebrate your journey and the small steps you take each day toward a healthier, more balanced life.

Continuing Your Somatic Journey

Healing is not a destination; it's a continuous process. Think of it as an evolving path rather than a straight line. There will be days when you feel immense progress and others when setbacks occur. This is entirely normal. Embracing this evolving nature of healing is crucial. Be patient with yourself and understand that each step contributes to your overall growth, no matter how small. Accepting that setbacks are part of the process can lessen the frustration and encourage a more compassionate approach to your healing. It's the journey that matters more than the destination.

Exploring advanced somatic practices can add depth to your healing as you progress. These practices might include new techniques or modalities outlined in Chapter 11 that you have yet to try.

For example, attending workshops or advanced Somatic Therapy sessions can offer fresh perspectives and tools. Seeking further education and training allows you to continually expand your knowledge and skills. This ongoing learning keeps your practice dynamic and engaging. It also ensures that you remain adaptable and can incorporate new methods that better suit your evolving needs.

Connecting with a supportive community remains vital.

These platforms often provide access to a wealth of resources and a network of individuals committed to continual growth.

Goal Setting Works for Somatic Practices

Setting long-term goals is another crucial aspect of sustaining your healing. These goals help you maintain focus and direction.

Here's the process:

1. Begin by identifying your personal and professional aspirations. What do you hope to achieve through your somatic practices?

2. Create a vision board or action plan. This can be incredibly motivating.

3. Visualize your goals to help make them feel more tangible and attainable. For instance, you might set goals for deeper emotional healing or professional development within the field of Somatic Therapy.

4. Break these goals into manageable steps to ensure steady progress and to keep yourself motivated.

Imagine setting a goal to deepen your emotional healing. This could involve committing to daily Meditation, attending monthly somatic workshops, and Journaling about your emotional experiences.

On the professional side, you might aim to complete advanced certification in Somatic Therapy. This could include enrolling in specialized courses, attending relevant conferences, and seeking mentorship from experienced practitioners. Each step, no matter how small, brings you closer to your long-term aspirations.

To help you stay on track:

1. Consider creating a detailed action plan.

2. Write down each goal and the steps required to achieve it.

3. Allocate specific timelines for each step and regularly review your progress.

This structured approach ensures that you remain focused and can adjust your plan as needed. Remember, the healing journey is not about perfection but consistent effort and progress.

Visual Element: Vision Board Exercise

A vision board can be a powerful tool for setting and visualizing your long-term goals.

Here's how to create one:

1. Gather materials You'll need a large piece of paper or a bulletin board, magazines, scissors, glue, and markers.

2. Reflect on your goals. Consider what you want to achieve in your somatic journey. These goals could be personal, professional, or a mix of both.

3. Find images for words. Look through magazines and cut out pictures and words that resonate with your goals.

4. Arrange and glue: Arrange these cutouts on your board in a way that inspires and motivates you. Glue them down once you're happy with the layout.

5. Add personal touches: use markers to write affirmations, quotes, or other words that inspire you.

6. Display your vision board. Place it somewhere you'll see it daily, constantly reminding you of your aspirations.

By integrating advanced practices, staying connected with a supportive community, and setting clear long-term goals, you create a robust framework for your ongoing healing. This approach ensures that your journey remains dynamic, fulfilling, and ever evolving. Remember, healing is not a linear process but a continuous path of growth and self-discovery.

Reflecting on Progress: The Importance of Self-Assessment

The process of healing requires dedication and a keen sense of self-awareness. Self-assessment plays a crucial role in this journey, acting as both a compass and a mirror. It helps you gain insights into your personal growth, highlighting areas where you've made strides and pinpointing aspects that need more attention. This ongoing reflection enhances your self-awareness and mindfulness, aligning you with your goals.

Imagine using regular self-assessment to evaluate how far you've come. It's like using a map to track your route, ensuring you're on the right path and making necessary adjustments.

Reflective Journaling

As stated previously, a practical technique for self-assessment is Reflective Journaling. Writing about your experiences and insights can be incredibly revealing. It allows you to document your emotional and physical states, providing a tangible record of your progress. Specific patterns emerge, helping you understand triggers and responses.

Body Scans with Reflection

Another effective method is conducting Body Scans with a focused reflection on changes and improvements. Set aside time each month for a self-check-in, where you evaluate your emotional and physical well-being. This practice tracks your progress and deepens your connection with your body.

Various tools and resources are available to aid in self-assessment. Assessment questionnaires and checklists can provide a structured way to evaluate different aspects of your well-being. These tools often include questions that prompt you to reflect on your emotional state, physical sensations, and overall progress. Tracking apps and digital journals offer a modern, convenient way to monitor stress levels and mood fluctuations. Using an app to record daily entries can help you see trends over time, offering valuable insights into your mental and physical health.

Receiving feedback from your self-assessment into your ongoing practices is essential for continuous improvement. Adjust your routines and techniques based on the insights you gather.

For example, if certain Breathwork practices are less effective during high-stress periods, you might modify them or try new techniques. Seeking input from therapists or support groups can also provide external perspectives that enhance your self-assessment. Sharing observations with a supportive community can lead to valuable advice and encouragement. This collaborative approach ensures that your healing practices remain dynamic and responsive to your evolving needs.

Interactive Element: Monthly Self-Check-In Worksheet

Take a moment to complete this monthly self-check-in worksheet. Reflect on your progress and identify areas for improvement.

1. Emotional State

   ◦ How have you felt emotionally over the past month?

   ◦ What emotions have been most prominent?

   ◦ Have there been any significant emotional triggers?

2. Physical State

   ◦ How has your body felt over the past month?

   ◦ Have you noticed any changes in tension or discomfort?

   ◦ What physical sensations have been most noticeable?

3. Progress and Setbacks

- What progress have you made towards your goals?

- Have there been any setbacks or challenges?

- How did you respond to these challenges?

4. Insights and Adjustments

- What insights have you gained from your self-assessment?

- What adjustments can you make to your routines and practices?

- How can you seek support from your community?

By regularly engaging in self-assessment, you can ensure that your healing journey remains aligned with your goals. This practice provides insights into making informed adjustments and enhancing well-being. Remember, the aim is not perfection but continuous growth and improvement.

Celebrating your successes, no matter how small, is crucial for motivation and positive reinforcement. It boosts self-esteem and confidence, making you feel capable and empowered. Recognizing and celebrating even small achievements reinforces positive behaviors and habits, creating a cycle of success and motivation.

For example, acknowledging that you took time to meditate every day for a week can significantly boost your confidence and encourage you to continue the practice.

Celebrating Progress

There are many creative and meaningful ways to celebrate your progress and milestones:

- One effective method is creating a Success Journal or scrapbook. This can be a physical book where you jot down achievements, paste photos, or add mementos that symbolize your progress.

- Sharing your achievements with loved ones or support groups is another powerful way to celebrate. Their encouragement and pride can amplify your sense of accomplishment.

- Hosting a small gathering to celebrate personal milestones can also be incredibly rewarding. For instance, inviting close friends for a cozy evening to celebrate a year of consistent practice can provide joy and motivation.

Don't Forget to Reflect

Reflecting on your achievements is equally important. Take time to write about your personal growth and the lessons you've learned. This practice helps solidify your progress and provides insights into your journey.

Creating a visual timeline of your progress can also be a powerful tool. This could be a simple chart or a more creative visual representation of your journey. Reflecting on the transformation in your emotional regulation over time, for example, can provide a clear picture of how far you've come and remind you of the positive changes in your life.

What's the Next Step?

Planning for future growth is the next step. Use the momentum from your celebrations and reflections to set new goals. Think about what you want to achieve next in your healing journey. These goals can be short-term and long-term, encompassing various aspects of your life. Write them down and create a plan to achieve them. Setting new goals helps maintain your focus and provides a sense of direction.

For example, set a goal to deepen your Meditation practice or attend a Somatic Therapy workshop. Planning for future growth ensures you continue evolving and progressing, keeping your healing journey dynamic and fulfilling.

Here are the summary charts for this chapter:

Practice	Ease of Practice	Time Commitment
Core Somatic Practices	Easy	5–10 mins
Balancing Activities	Moderate	Varies
Joyful Activities	Easy	Varies
Time in Nature	Easy	30 mins
Mindful Relaxation	Easy	5–10 mins
Morning Meditation	Easy	10 mins
Mindful Stretching	Easy	5–10 mins
Daily Breathwork	Easy	5 mins
Evening Body Scan	Easy	5–10 mins
Journaling	Easy	10–15 mins
Setting Goals	Moderate	Varies
Vision Board Creation	Easy	Varies
Tracking Progress	Easy	10 mins
Celebrating Milestones	Easy	5–10 mins
Reflective Journaling	Easy	10 mins
Monthly Self-Check-Ins	Moderate	10–15 mins
Body Scans with Reflection	Moderate	15 mins
Feedback Loops	Moderate	5–10 mins

Practice	Reduces Stress	Improves Emotional Regulation	Prevents Burnout	Enhances Overall Well-Being
Core Somatic Practices (Breathwork, Body Scan)	✓	✓	✓	✓
Balancing Active and Restorative Activities	✓	✓	✓	✓
Incorporating Joyful Activities	✓	✓	✓	✓
Time in Nature	✓			✓
Mindful Relaxation	✓	✓	✓	✓

Practice	Provides Focus	Boosts Motivation	Encourages Growth
Morning Meditation	✓	✓	✓
Mindful Stretching (Lunch Break)	✓	✓	✓
Daily Breathwork	✓	✓	✓
Evening Body Scan	✓	✓	✓
Journaling		✓	✓
Joyful Activities (Hobbies, Nature Walks)		✓	✓

Practice	Provides Focus	Boosts Motivation	Encourages Growth
Setting Realistic Goals	✓	✓	✓
Vision Board Creation	✓	✓	✓
Tracking Progress	✓	✓	✓
Celebrating Milestones	✓	✓	✓

Tool/Practice	Tracks Progress	Identifies Challenges	Supports Continuous Improvement
Reflective Journaling	✓	✓	✓
Body Scans with Reflection	✓	✓	✓
Monthly Self-Check-Ins	✓	✓	✓
Feedback Loops	✓	✓	✓

CONCLUSION

As we reach the end of Body Wisdom through Somatic Therapy, I want to reiterate this book's vision and purpose. My aim has always been to offer a compassionate and practical guide for you to reconnect with your inner wisdom. These pages have given you the tools to manage stress, rebuild resilience, and foster deep body awareness.

Somatic Therapy holds a unique and crucial place in the world of healing. Unlike traditional therapy methods that often focus solely on the mind, Somatic Therapy integrates the body, recognizing it as a vital part of our emotional and psychological landscape. This approach is transformative because it acknowledges that stress, trauma, and unresolved emotions are stored not just in our minds but also in our bodies. We can process and release these burdens by tuning into our physical sensations, leading to profound healing and well-being.

As I mentioned, I want to provide a bridge between the Christian world and these therapies. In my church experience, there has been a disconnect between these therapies and traditional Christian practices. I hope that this book enables the Christian world to more fully embrace all that our Creator made available to us through the magnificent creation that our bodies are. I have come to think of these as God's technology for wholeness.

In the Introduction of this book, I mentioned I was on sabbatical to figure out what the role the sons of God in Romans 8:19 was to creation. Writing this book has helped me immensely to determine this answer in the context of Somatic Therapy.

My final thoughts on this are that there are six ways that Somatic Therapy is tied to the sons of God:

1. <u>The sons of God are those who can hear Him.</u> Practicing somatic techniques helps individuals cultivate a sense of being children of God through the physical sensation of peace, presence, and connection, clear results of the techniques.

2. Romans 8:19 speaks of creation's longing, which could symbolize a broken or incomplete state awaiting restoration. Healing trauma and emotional pain stored in the body is often addressed by Somatic Therapy. When these are healed, our true identity is revealed, and restoration occurs in the person. <u>With Somatic Therapy, they can now much more fully embody their divine identity.</u>

3. Mind-body-spirit integration is consistent with the biblical theme of holistic restoration. We are not just our bodies or just our minds. We are mind-body-spirit, three in one. Somatic therapy integrates physical awareness with mental and emotional healing. <u>The sons of God could be those who manifest a holistic, integrated life that reflects divine purpose, healing not only themselves but impacting all creation.</u>

4. Scripture mentions creation eagerly awaiting this revelation, suggesting a deep interconnection between humanity and the physical world. <u>When healing and self-awareness in individuals from Somatic Therapy ripples out to creation, it symbolizes a mutual restoration process.</u>

5. Breathwork, Grounding, or Movement techniques could serve as practical ways for believers to embody spiritual truths, living out their identity as the "sons of God" in tangible, physical ways. <u>This embodiment then might resonate with creation, fulfilling its longing for the sons of God to be revealed in action, not just in theology.</u>

6. Romans 8:19 uses the term of "eager longing," which Somatic Therapy could explore as a felt experience. How does longing manifest in the body? Perhaps it is in <u>recognizing and aligning with these sensations that deepens the understanding of what it means for creation and humanity to anticipate fulfillment.</u>

By combining the theological framework of scripture with the experiential insights of Somatic Therapy, this approach could provide a richer understanding of how the "sons of God" are revealed, not only in spiritual terms but also in how they embody divine identity in creation.

The Somatic Techniques Themselves

Throughout the book, we've delved into various aspects of Somatic Therapy. We've explored the foundational principles and scientific backing, including trauma's neurobiology and the vagus nerve's importance in stress regulation. We've differentiated Somatic Therapy from traditional talk therapy, emphasizing its unique benefits for managing trauma and chronic stress.

Practical exercises have been a cornerstone of this journey. The exercises offer tangible ways to enhance body awareness and emotional regulation, from Body Scanning and Grounding techniques to advanced practices like Pendulation. We've also covered

Breathwork, Body Awareness practices, and daily Movement routines to release tension and build resilience.

The key takeaways from this book are simple yet profound. First, recognize the importance of tuning into your body. Your body holds wisdom that can guide you toward healing and peace. Incorporate somatic practices into your daily routine. Even a few minutes a day can make a significant difference. Utilize Grounding exercises, Breathwork, and Mindful movement to stay connected to the present moment and manage stress effectively.

As someone who has walked this path, I can personally attest to the transformative power of Somatic Therapy. My journey began in a state of disconnection with my body and high amounts of stress. Through consistent practice, I found a deeper connection to my body and a newfound sense of peace and spiritual vitality. I encourage you to embrace this journey with an open heart. Healing is not linear, but each step brings you closer to a more balanced and resilient self.

Hope For Your Future

Take your next steps with confidence. Apply the techniques you've learned, seek support from your community, and continue exploring somatic practices.

In closing, I want to leave you with a final thought. Imagine your own world where you can rise above trauma and have inner peace. Then, imagine a world where everyone rises above trauma, cultivates inner peace, and thrives, where everyone learns to manage their emotions. This vision is within our reach, one mindful breath and one Body Scan at a time.

Thank you for allowing me to be a part of your journey. Remember, you have the power to heal, to reconnect with your body, and to transform your life. Here's to your continued growth and well-being.

Keeping the Wisdom Alive

Now that you have everything you need to manage stress, rebuild resilience, and nurture a deeper connection to your body, it's time to pass on your newfound knowledge and help other readers discover the same support and guidance.

By leaving your honest opinion of this book on Amazon, you'll show other readers seeking healing and growth where they can find the tools they need. Together, we can pass on our passion for Somatic Therapy and make it accessible to more people.

Thank you for your support. Somatic Therapy thrives when we share what we've learned and experienced—and by leaving your review, you're helping me to do just that.

Scan the QR code or visit the link below to leave your review on Amazon:

https://www.amazon.com/review/review-your-purchases/?asin=B0DSLWC8KG

Warmly,
Grace Bailey

APPENDIX 1.

Glossary

BELOW IS A LIST of the exercises covered in this book with a brief description.

Body Scanning

Body Scanning is a foundational exercise in Somatic Therapy. It involves moving one's attention through different areas of one's body to notice and release tension.

- Imagine you're using a mental flashlight, slowly moving it from the top of your head down to your toes. This exercise helps you become more aware of physical sensations and can reveal areas where you're holding onto stress. By regularly practicing Body Scanning, you can develop a deeper connection with your body and learn to recognize early signs of tension before they escalate.

- Body Mapping involves visualizing your body and marking areas where you feel tension, pain, or other sensations. This practice helps you become more aware of your physical state and can reveal patterns related to stress and emotions. By regularly updating your body map, you can track changes over time and gain new insights into your body's responses.

- Body Awareness exercises focus on tuning into your bodily sensations and becoming more aware of your physical state. This could involve simple activities like noticing your breath or paying attention to the feeling of your feet on the ground. These exercises help you develop a deeper connection with your body and can reveal areas where you hold tension or stress.

- Progressive Muscle Relaxation involves tensing and then relaxing different muscle groups. This practice helps release physical tension and promotes overall relaxation. By systematically working through each muscle group, you can become more aware of where you hold tension and learn to let it go. This exercise is particularly effective for reducing stress and improving sleep quality.

- Self-massage involves using your hands or a massage tool to apply gentle pressure to different body areas. This practice helps release muscle tension, improve circulation, and promote relaxation. Self-massage can be done anywhere and anytime, making it an accessible way to care for your body and reduce stress.

- Bioenergetics exercises include full-body Shakes and expansive Stretches to break up stagnant energy and improve flow. These more dynamic exercises can help release deep-seated tension. For example, Shaking out your limbs or doing a Full-Body Stretch can invigorate your body and mind, leaving you feeling more energized and less burdened by stress. Bioenergetics exercises are a great way to revitalize your body and clear your mind.

Breathwork Exercises

Breathwork exercises like Box Breathing and Belly Breathing are powerful tools for calming the nervous system and staying present.

- Box Breathing involves inhaling for four counts, holding for four, exhaling for four, and holding again for four.

- Belly Breathing, or Diaphragmatic Breathing, involves taking deep breaths that expand your abdomen rather than your chest. These exercises help regulate your body's stress response and can be particularly useful during moments of high anxiety.

Containment with Safe Touch

Containment with safe touch uses compassionate physical contact to create a sense of safety and stability. This might involve hugging yourself, touching your heart, or gently massaging your shoulders. These simple gestures can profoundly impact your emotional state, providing comfort and reassurance. Safe Touch exercises help you feel more grounded and connected to your body, especially during emotional distress.

Emotional Labeling

Emotional Labeling involves identifying and naming your emotions as they arise. This practice helps create distance between you and your emotions, making them easier to manage. Acknowledging your feelings can reduce their intensity and gain greater control over your emotional responses. Emotional Labeling is a simple yet powerful tool for emotional regulation and self-awareness.

Emotional Processing Exercises

Emotional Processing exercises involve activities that help you explore and understand your emotions. This could include writing about your feelings, talking to a trusted friend, or engaging in creative activities like drawing or painting. These exercises help you process and release emotions, promoting healing and well-being.

Gentle Body Movements

Gentle body movements include yoga, free dance, Targeted Stretches, and Walking Meditations. These exercises help release stored tension and improve overall body awareness. Unlike intense workouts, Gentle Movements are about tuning into your body and moving in ways that feel good. They can be done anywhere and anytime, making them an accessible way to reconnect with your body throughout the day.

Mindful Stretching combines Body Awareness with Gentle Stretches to promote relaxation and flexibility. This practice involves moving slowly and deliberately, paying attention to the sensations in your muscles and joints. By stretching mindfully, you can release physical tension and improve your well-being. Mindful Stretching is a great way to start or end your day, helping you feel more connected to your body.

Grounding Techniques

Grounding techniques use sensory experiences to anchor you to the present moment. These exercises can be as simple as feeling the texture of a soft blanket, noticing the coolness of a breeze, or focusing on the sensation of your feet touching the ground. Grounding helps calm the nervous system, making it easier to manage stress and anxiety. It's like hitting the reset button for your mind and body, helping you feel more stable and centered.

Grounding techniques also refers to the correction of EMF in your home. This involves removing dirty electricity and harmful electromagnetic fields from internet routers, SMART devices, cell phone towers close to our homes, and devices such as electronic screens of any kind in our bedroom at night. When EMF is restored to one that is consistent with good health, many symptoms the body and mind experience will go away and you will feel more stable in many ways.

Journaling

Journaling is a powerful tool for emotional processing and self-reflection. Writing about your thoughts and feelings can help you gain clarity and insight, reduce stress, and improve your overall mental health. There are many different types of journaling, from

Expressive Journal writing to Gratitude Journaling. Each offers unique benefits and can be tailored to your personal needs and preferences.

Expressive Journal writing involves writing freely about your thoughts and feelings without worrying about grammar, spelling, or structure. This practice helps you process emotions and experiences, providing relief and clarity. By expressing yourself honestly and openly, you can gain new insights and perspectives on your experiences, promoting emotional healing.

Gratitude Journaling involves regularly writing about the things you are grateful for. This practice helps shift your focus from negative to positive aspects of your life, promoting a more optimistic outlook. Gratitude Journaling can improve mood, reduce stress, and enhance mind-body wellness. It's a simple yet powerful way to cultivate a positive mindset.

Affirmations are positive statements you repeat to reinforce a positive mindset and build self-confidence. These statements can be tailored to your personal goals and values, helping you focus on your strengths and potential. Regularly practicing affirmations can counteract negative self-talk and promote a more positive and empowered outlook.

Meditation

Meditation involves focusing your mind on a specific object, thought, or activity to achieve a state of mental clarity and emotional calm. There are many different types of Meditation, from Mindfulness to Loving Kindness. Each offers unique benefits and can be tailored to your needs and preferences. Meditation helps reduce stress, improve focus, and promotes physical and mental health.

- Loving Kindness Meditation involves silently repeating phrases of goodwill and compassion towards yourself and others. This practice helps cultivate a positive and compassionate mindset, reducing anger and resentment. Regularly practicing Loving Kindness Meditation can improve your relationships and promote emotional well-being.

- Mindfulness Meditation involves focusing on the present moment and observing your thoughts and sensations without judgment. This practice helps you stay grounded and aware, reducing the impact of stress and anxiety. Regularly practicing mindfulness meditation can improve your mental clarity and emotional stability.

- Walking Meditation combines the mindfulness of traditional meditation with the physical activity of walking. It involves walking slowly and deliberately, focusing on the sensation of each step. This practice helps you stay present and grounded, providing a calming and centering experience. Walking Meditation can be particularly effective in natural settings, where you can also connect with the sights and sounds of your environment.

- Biblical Meditation. One that I have used in the past is Transformation Prayer sessions. This involves visualizing a traumatic event and then asking," Where was Jesus when this was happening?" I was amazed with the results of this after using it to process different traumatic events. In every one of them, Jesus has always been there protecting me. I have never been alone during those times. When you can view an event knowing that Jesus was there the whole time, the event loses much of its power to traumatize and keep you in a negative cycle. If you want to explore this practice further, more information is available at this website: https://www.transformationprayer.org/about-us/

Mindful Eating

Mindful Eating is about paying attention to the sensory experience of eating. It involves slowing down and savoring each bite, noticing your food's flavors, textures, and aromas. This practice can help you develop a healthier relationship with food, reducing overeating and promoting better digestion. By eating mindfully, you can also become more aware of your body's hunger and fullness cues, leading to more balanced eating habits.

Pendulation

Pendulation is the practice of oscillating between states of tension and relaxation. It involves moving your focus between a part of your body that feels tight or uncomfortable and a part that feels calm or neutral. This back-and-forth movement helps your nervous system learn how to regulate itself more effectively. Pendulation can be particularly helpful for managing intense emotions, allowing you to experience discomfort without becoming overwhelmed.

Resourcing

Resourcing involves tapping into your personal experiences and memories related to joy, peace, and strength during turbulent times. This could be as simple as recalling a happy memory, visualizing a peaceful place, or thinking about someone who makes you feel loved and supported. Resourcing helps build emotional strength by reminding you of the positive aspects of your life. It's like having a mental toolkit of comforting thoughts and images you can draw upon whenever you need them. It also gives you a deep sense of gratitude because you have had dozens of experiences that were positive, and provides hope because it's certainly possible to have more in the future.

Rhythmic Movement

Engaging in rhythmic actions, such as Swaying or Strolling at a relaxed pace, connects with your body's inherent rhythms. These movements help synchronize your body and mind, promoting a sense of calm and relaxation. Rhythmic movement can be especially effective when combined with soothing music or sounds from nature. It's a gentle way to release tension and reconnect with your body's natural rhythms.

Self-Regulation Techniques

Self-regulation techniques focus on building emotional control through Mindfulness, Breathwork, and Guided Visualizations. These practices help you manage your emotional responses more effectively, reducing the impact of stress and anxiety on your daily life. Engaging in Mindfulness exercises, such as focusing on Breathing or tuning into a particular sensation, supports staying present and grounded. Guided Visualizations, where you imagine a calming scene or situation, can provide a mental escape from stress.

Self-Compassion Exercises

Self-compassion exercises focus on treating yourself with kindness and understanding. This could involve writing a letter to yourself, acknowledging your struggles, and offering encouragement. Self-compassion helps counteract negative self-talk and promotes a more positive and supportive relationship with yourself. Practicing self-compassion can build emotional strength and improve your all-around wellness.

Visualization Techniques

Visualization engages with positive mental images to initiate healing and tranquility. It involves imagining a peaceful place or a positive outcome, using all your senses to make the image as vivid as possible.

- Visualization can reduce stress, improve focus, and promote a sense of calm. It's like creating a mental sanctuary that you can visit whenever you need a break from the pressures of daily life. Safe Space Visualization involves imagining a place where you feel completely secure and at ease. This could be a real place you've been to or an entirely imagined setting.

Visualizing this safe space allows you to create a mental retreat that provides comfort and security. This exercise is particularly helpful during times of stress or anxiety, offering a calming escape that you can access anytime.

- Guided Imagery involves listening to a recording or following a script that leads you through calming visualizations. This practice helps reduce stress and promote relaxation by engaging your imagination. Guided imagery can be particularly effective for those who find it difficult to meditate or relax on their own. It provides a structured and supportive way to access the benefits of visualization.

7-Step Somatic Exercise

This comprehensive exercise helps process triggers and traumatic memories through breathing, visualization, and movement.

It involves seven steps:

1. Find a safe space.

2. Ground yourself.

3. Identify a trigger.

4. Focus on your breath.

5. Visualize a calming image.

6. Move gently to release tension.

7. Reflect on the experience.

Each step is designed to guide you through processing difficult emotions and memories in a controlled and supportive way. This exercise can be beneficial for those dealing with trauma, as it provides a structured approach to working through challenging experiences.

APPENDIX 2.

Resources

Somatic Therapy

Be Your Best Self & Thrive website. Somatic Healing Practices and Techniques: Holistic Therapy Explained. Updated July 9, 2024. Accessed online October 2024. https://www.bybsandthrive.com/post/somatic-healing-practices-and-techniques.

Kirstein, Mona, PhD. 12 Effective Somatic Therapy Exercises for Holistic Healing. October 2023. Accessed online October 2024. https://www.monakirstein.com/somatic-therapy-exercises/

Leo. Somatic Therapy: How It Can Help You Heal Faster. Oct. 7, 2023. – Psychology. Accessed online October 2024.

Maierhofer, Brian. Somatic Therapy. Accessed online November 2024. https://threadreaderapp.com/thread/1846595500566294888.html

Monimawellness.com. Somatic Therapy in San Diego | Somatic Experiencing Therapy. Accessed online November 2024. https://www.monimawellness.com/our-approach/somatic-experience-therapy

RefugeAcu website. How Somatic Therapy Changes The Brain. https://www.refugeacu.com/blog/how-somatic-therapy-changes-the-brain.

Salamon, Maureen. What is Somatic Therapy? July 7, 2023. Harvard Health Publishing. Harvard Medical School website. Accessed online October 2024. https://www.health.harvard.edu/blog/what-is-somatic-therapy-202307072951

TalkHealthThrive. Unveiling the Power of Somatic Therapy. Accessed online November 2024.

https://talkhealthrive.com/post/unveiling-the-power-of-somatic-therapy-a-pathway-to-healing-from-within

Somatic Experiencing

Brom, Danny, et al. Somatic Experiencing for Posttraumatic Stress Disorder: A Randomized Controlled Outcome. J Trauma Stress. 2017 Jun 6:30(3):304-312. https://www.ncbi.nlm.nih.gov/pmc/articles/PMC5518443

Emoverlic.com. Somatic Experiencing, Starting Therapy. June 16, 2023. Accessed online October 2024. https://emoverellc.com/2023/06/16/benefits-of-online-somatic-experiencing-therapy/

Kuhfub M, Maldei T, Hetmanek A, and Baumann, N. Somatic Experiencing–Effectiveness and Key Factors of a Body-Oriented Trauma Therapy Scoping Literature Review. Eur J Psychotraumatol 2021 Jul 12; 12(1): 1929023. https://pmc.ncbi.nlm.nih.gov/articles/PMC8276649

Ramirez-Duran, Daniela. Somatic Experiencing Therapy: 10 Best Exercises & Examples. Nov. 11, 2020. https://positivepsychology.com/somatic-experiencing Accessed online October 2024.

Ross, Sarah. Resourcing, Pendulation and Titration: Practices from Somatic Experiencing®. January 3, 2018. Sarah Ross PhD website. Accessed online October 2024. https://sarahrossphd.com/resourcing-pendulation-titration-practices-somatic-experiencing

SEI Communications. Real Stories of SE™. Oct. 3, 2022. Somatic Experiencing International website. Accessed online October 2024. https://traumahealing.org/real-stories-of-se/

Somatic Experiencing International. Somatic Experiencing Practitioner Directory. https://directory.traumahealing.org

Yalom, Victor and Yalom, Marie-Helen. Peter Levine on Somatic Experiencing. Accessed online October 2024. https://www.psychotherapy.net/interview/interview-peter-levine

Body Scan and Body Awareness

Mehling, W.E., et al. Body Awareness: A Phenomenological Inquiry Into the Common Ground of Mind-Body Therapies. Accessed online October 2024. Philos Ethics Humanit Med. 2011 Apr 7;6:6. https://pmc.ncbi.nlm.nih.gov/articles/PMC3096919

Scott, Elizabeth, PhD. What is Body Scan Meditation? Release Tension with This Targeted Meditation Technique. Updated on Feb. 12, 2024. Accessed online October

2024. VeryWellMind website.
https://www.verywellmind.com/body-scan-meditation-why-and-how-3144782

Breathing

Cronkleton, Emily. 10 Breathing Exercises to Try When You're Feeling Stressed. Updated on May 17, 2024. Healthline website. Accessed online September 2024. https://www.healthline.com/health/breathing-exercise

Eboost.com. Alternate Nostril Breathe Your Way Into a Stress Free Monday. Accessed online October 2024. https://blog.eboost.com/2017/03/alternate-nostril-breathe-way-stress-free-monday/

MasterClass. Holotropic Breathing: All About Holotropic Breathwork Techniques. Sept. 15, 2022. Accessed online September 2024. https://www.masterclass.com/articles/holotropic-breathing

Chronic Pain

NIH. Mind and Body Approaches for Chronic Pain. NCCIH Clinical Digest for Health Professionals. August 2019. Accessed online October 2024. https://www.nccih.nih.gov/health/providers/digest/mind-and-body-approaches-for-chronic-pain

Noorani A, Hung PS, Zhang JY, Sohng K, Laperriere N, Moayedi M, Hodaie M. Pain Relief Reverses Hippocampal Abnormalities in Trigeminal Neuralgia. J Pain. 2022 Jan;23(1):141-155. Doi: 10.1016/j.jpain.2021.07.004. Epub 2021 Aug 8. PMID: 34380093.

Sibille, KT, et al. Increasing Neuroplasticity to Bolster Chronic Pain Treatment. J Pain. 2016 Feb 2;17(3):275-281. https://www.ncbi.nlm.nih.gov/pmc/articles/PMC4824292

Southern Pain and Neurological. 5 Proven Relaxation Techniques to Reduce Chronic Pain. April 4, 2023. Accessed online October 2024. https://southernpainclinic.com/blog/5-proven-relaxation-techniques-to-reduce-chronic-pain/

Zhao W, Zhao L, Chang X, Lu X, Tu Y. Elevated dementia risk, cognitive decline, and hippocampal atrophy in multisite chronic pain. Proc Natl Acad Sci U S A. 2023 Feb 28;120(9):e2215192120. Doi: 10.1073/pnas.2215192120. Epub 2023 Feb 21. PMID: 36802440; PMCID: PMC9992778.

Embodiment

Madeson, Melissa, PhD. Embodiment Practices: How to Heal Through Movement. August 11, 2021. Accessed online September 2024. https://positivepsychology.com/embodiment-philosophy-practices

Emotional Wellness and Stress

Anwar, Yasmin. The 16 facial expressions most common to emotional situations worldwide. December 17, 2020. University of California. Accessed online November 2024. https://www.universityofcalifornia.edu/news/16-facial-expressions-most-common-emotional-situations-worldwide

Bay Area CBT Center. Somatic Experiencing in CBT: Enhancing Trauma Treatment. July 26, 2024. Bay Area CBT Center website. Accessed online September 2024. https://bayareacbtcenter.com/the-role-of-somatic-experiencing-in-cbt/

Calm.com. How to Create A Self-care Plan Personalized to Your Needs. Calm.com website. Accessed online October 2024. https://www.calm.com/blog/self-care-plan

Clapp, Jane. Body and Psyche: An Introduction to Jungian Somatics. Sept. 25, 2024. Accessed online October 2024. https://www.jungarchademy.com/clapp1

Discover Healing. Discover Energy Healing with the Emotion Code®, Body Code™, and Belief Code®. Accessed online October 2024. https://discoverhealing.com

Familydoctor.org. Mind/Body Connection: How Your Emotions Affect Your Health. Updated December 2022. Accessed online October 2024. https://familydoctor.org/mindbody-connection-how-your-emotions-affect-your-health/

Klynn, Bethany. Emotional Regulation: Skills, Exercises, and Strategies. June 22, 2021. BetterUp website. Accessed online October 2024. https://www.betterup.com/blog/emotional-regulation-skills

Mayo Clinic. Exercise and stress: Get Moving to Manage Stress. Accessed online October 2024. https://www.mayoclinic.org/healthy-lifestyle/stress-management/in-depth/exercise-and-stress/art-20044469#:~:text=Examples%20include%20walking%2C%20stair%20climbing,a%20yoga%20video%20at%20home

Mental Health First Aid USA. The Importance of Having a Support System. August 6, 2020. Accessed online September 2024. https://www.mentalhealthfirstaid.org/2020/08/the-importance-of-having-a-support-system

Nelson, Bradley. The Emotion Code. Blinkist website. Accessed online October 2024. https://www.blinkist.com/en/books/the-emotion-code-en.

NIH. Your Healthiest Self. Emotional Wellness Toolkit. Accessed online October 2024. https://www.nih.gov/health-information/emotional-wellness-toolkit#:~:text=To%20build%20healthy%20support%20systems,reading%2C%20hiking%2C%20or%20painting

Robinson, Karen, Trauma Recovery Expert. Episode 104: Transforming Trauma with Love and Loyalty: Marinda Dennis' Uplifting Path to Recovery. HealThriveDream, A Mother Daughter Company. Accessed online October 2024. https://www.healthrivedream.com/podcast/episode104

Simic, G., et al. Understanding Emotions: Origins and Roles of the Amygdala. Biomolecules. 2021 May 31;11(6):823. https://pmc.ncbi.nlm.nih.gov/articles/PMC8228195

Verghese, Abraham. Spirituality and Mental Health. Indian J Psychiatry. 2008 Oct-Dec;50(4): 233-237. https://www.ncbi.nlm.nih.gov/pmc/articles/PMC2755140

Grounding

Jain, Mansi. How to Stay in the Present Moment - 5 Practical Tips that Works! Nov. 22, 2021. Mindsutra website. Accessed online October 2024. https://www.mindsutra.in/post/how-to-stay-in-the-present-moment-5-practical-tips-that-works

Raypole, Crystal. 30 Grounding Techniques to Quiet Distressing Thoughts. Healthline website. Accessed online October 2024. https://www.healthline.com/health/grounding-techniques

Journaling

Sutton, Jeremy. 5 Benefits of Journaling for Mental Health. May 14, 2018. Accessed online September 2024. https://positivepsychology.com/benefits-of-journaling

Meditation

RelaxLikeABoss.com. Can I Meditate Lying Down? Exploring the Benefits and Techniques. Accessed online October 2024. https://relaxlikeaboss.com/meditate-lying-down/

Memory

Hainmueller T, Bartos M. Dentate gyrus circuits for encoding, retrieval and discrimination of episodic memories. Nat Rev Neurosci. 2020 Mar;21(3):153-168. doi: 10.1038/s41583-019-0260-z. Epub 2020 Feb 10. PMID: 32042144; PMCID: PMC7115869.

Nokia MS, Penttonen M. Rhythmic Memory Consolidation in the Hippocampus. Front Neural Circuits. 2022 Apr 1;16:885684. doi: 10.3389/fncir.2022.885684. PMID: 35431819; PMCID: PMC9011342.

Mindfulness

Recovery Protocols website. 9 Best Practices for Cultivating Mind-Body Connection Through Mindfulness. Accessed online September 2024. https://www.recoveryprotocols.com/9-best-practices-for-cultivating-mind-body-connection-through-mindfulness-2

Movement

Hadley, Heidi. What is the Difference between Stretching and Pandiculation? Total Somatics website. Accessed online October 2024. https://totalsomatics.com/what-is-the-difference-between-stretching-and-pandiculation/

Savvidou, P., & Myers, H. (2016). Movement And Wellness Training For Musicians: A Case Study Report. MTNA e - Journal, 7(4), 22-36. https://www.proquest.com/openview/e5ca30eb4bbd34f136119912bfcc7ded/1?pq-origsite=gscholar&cbl=726357

Scatty. 5 Dangers of Sitting Too Much: How Sedentary Behavior Affects Your Health. May 17, 2023. Accessed online October 2024. https://scatty.com/5-dangers-of-sitting-too-much-how-sedentary-behavior-affects-your-health/

Somatic Movement Center. How to Get the Most Out of Clinical Somatic Exercises. Somatic Movement Center website. Accessed online October 2024. https://somaticmovementcenter.com/somatic-exercises-learn-hanna-somatic-exercises/

Young, Courtenay. The History and Development of Body-Psychotherapy: The American Legacy of Wilhelm Reich l. Body Movement and Dance in Psychotherapy 3(1), Mar 2008. Accessed online October 2024. https://www.researchgate.net/publication/237676251_The_History_and_Development_of_Body-Psychotherapy_The_American_Legacy_of_Wilhelm_Reich1

Nutrition, Sleep, and Other Habits

Alexis, A.C., MSPH, RDN. 10 Foods and Drinks with Caffeine. June 14, 2021. Reviewed by Sade Meeks, MS, RD. Healthline website. Accessed online November 2024. https://www.healthline.com/nutrition/foods-with-caffeine

iAwakeTechnologies.com. Transformative Sound Technologies for an Evolving World. Accessed online October 2024. https://www.iawaketechnologies.com/

Leafy-Clafoutis website. Evening Routine: Get Ready for Sleep. Last updated: March 22, 2023. Accessed online October 2024. https://leafy-clafoutis-690980.netlify.app/checklists/evening/evening-routine-get-ready-for-sleep

NIH News in Health website. Creating Healthy Habits Make Better Choices Easier. March 2018. Accessed online October 2024. https://newsinhealth.nih.gov/2018/03/creating-healthy-habits

NIH News in Health website. Good Sleep for Good Health. April 2021. Accessed online October 2024. https://newsinhealth.nih.gov/2021/04/good-sleep-good-health#:~:text=Everything%20from%20blood%20vessels%20to,during%20sleep%2C%E2%80%9D%20he%20explains

Selhub, Eva, M.D. Nutritional Psychiatry: Your Brain on Food. Sept. 18, 2022. Harvard Health Publishing. Harvard Medical School. Accessed online October 2024. https://www.health.harvard.edu/blog/nutritional-psychiatry-your-brain-on-food-201511168626.

WebMD. Foods High in Tryptophan. WebMD website. Medically reviewed by Zilpha Sheikh, MD on Nov. 13, 2023. Accessed November 2024. https://www.webmd.com/diet/foods-high-in-tryptophan

Pendulation

Third Nature Therapy. Uncovering the Role of Pendulation in Trauma Therapy. Accessed online October 2024. https://www.thirdnaturetherapy.com/blog/what-is-pendulation#:~:text=Nervous%20System%20Regulation%3A%20Pendulation%20helps,increases%20tolerance%20for%20distressing%20experiences

Polyvagal Theory

Lankford, Terri K., LPCS. Polyvagal Part 2: Vagal Tone & Our Vagal Brake. July 15, 2024. Accessed online Nov. 10, 2024.

https://www.riseandthrivecounseling.com/post/polyvagal-part-2-vagal-tone-our-vagal -brake

Mind By Design. Polyvagal Theory: 8 Co-Regulation Skills For Relationships. Mind By Design LLC website. Accessed online October 2024. https://mindbydesignllc.com/blog/polyvagal-theory-co-regulation

Porges SW. The Polyvagal Theory: New Insights into Adaptive Reactions of the Autonomic Nervous System. Cleve Clin J Med. 2009 Apr;76 Suppl 2(Suppl 2):S86-90. doi: 10.3949/ccjm.76.s2.17. PMID: 19376991; PMCID: PMC3108032.

Relaxation

Nunez, Kirsten. The Benefits of Progressive Muscle Relaxation and How to Do It. August 10, 2020. Healthline website. Accessed online October 2024. https://www.healthline.com/health/progressive-muscle-relaxatio

Resourcing

Holzmann, Maira. Healing From Trauma: The Power of Resourcing Techniques. May 18, 2023. Accessed online October 2024. https://somatictherapypartners.com/healing-from-trauma-the-power-of-resourcing-te chniques

Vibration

Chawla, G., et al. Effect of Whole-body Vibration on Depression, Anxiety, Stress and Quality of Life in College Students: A Randomized Control Trial. Man Med J. 2022 Jul 31;37(4):e408. https://pmc.ncbi.nlm.nih.gov/articles/PMC9396709

Visualization

Alvarez-Garcia C, Simsek Yaban Z. The Effects of Preoperative Guided Imagery Interventions on Preoperative Anxiety and Postoperative Pain: A Meta-analysis. Complement Ther Clin Pract. 2020 Feb: 38:101077. https://pubmed.ncbi.nlm.nih.gov/32056813

Giacobbi PR, Stabler M, et al. Guided Imagery for Arthritis and Other Rheumatic Diseases: A Systematic Review of Randomized Controlled Trials. Pain Manag Nurs. 2015 Jul 11;16(5):792-803. https://pmc.ncbi.nlm.nih.gov/articles/PMC4605831

Molinari G, Garcia-Palacios A, et al. The Power of Visualization: Back to the Future for Pain Management in Fibromyalgia Syndrome. Pain Med. 2018 Jul 1;19(7):1451-1468. https://pubmed.ncbi.nlm.nih.gov/29294081

Saleh A, Bachtiar SM, Sjattar E, and Abrar EA. The Effectiveness of Technical Guided Imagery on Pain Intensity Decreasing in Breast Cancer Patients. International Conference on Women and Societal Perspective on Quality of Life (WOSQUAL-2019), March 2020, 30(52), 45-48. https://www.elsevier.es/en-revista-enfermeria-clinica-35-articulo-the-effectiveness-technical-guided-imagery-S1130862119303249

Other

Shadow Self: Understand Your Dark Side And Find Your Light. Accessed online October 2024. https://rediscoveringsacredness.com/shadow-self-understand-your-dark-side-and-find-your-light

Heallist.com Sustainable Practices in Holistic Health: Trends for Eco-Friendly Healing. July 15, 2024. Accessed online October 2024. https://www.heallist.com/resources/blog/sustainable-practices-in-holistic-health-trends-for-eco-friendly-healing

Stanford Medicine. Self-Assessment. Evaluating Your Well-Being. Accessed online October 2024. https://wellmd.stanford.edu/self-assessment.html

www.ingramcontent.com/pod-product-compliance
Lightning Source LLC
Chambersburg PA
CBHW081533120626
46550CB00009B/2718